GUNS & GUN
COLLECTING

GUNS & GUN COLLECTING

De Witt Bailey   Ian Hogg
Geoffrey Boothroyd   Frederick Wilkinson

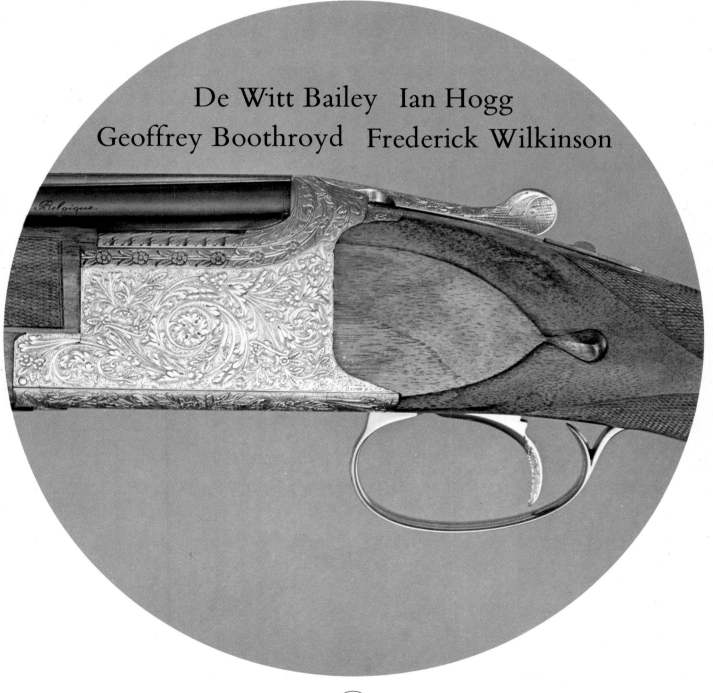

OCTOPUS BOOKS

First published in Great Britain in
1972 by Octopus Books Limited
59 Grosvenor Street, London W.1.

Book layout by
Artes Graphicae Ltd,
26 Harrison Street,
London W.C.1.

Produced by Mandarin Publishers Limited
77a Marble Road, North Point, Hong Kong
Printed in Hong Kong

CONTENTS

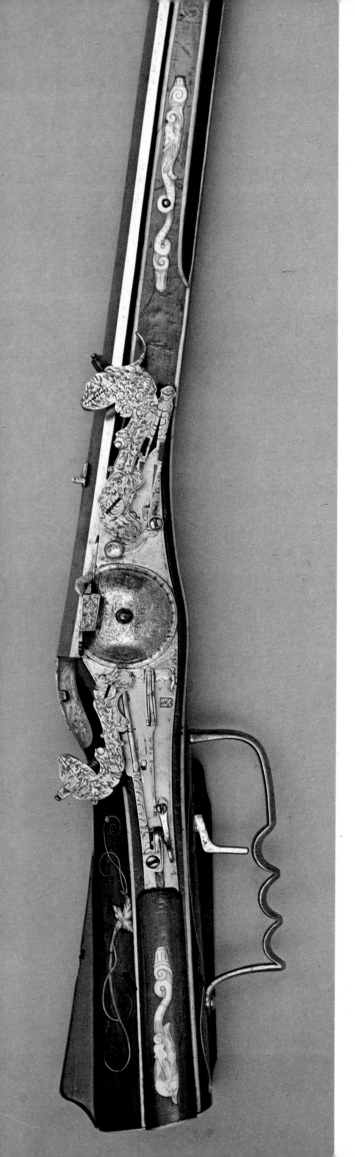

Right:
This is probably one of the latest non-oriental matchlocks known: a Spanish American example dated 1844. The brasswork is crudely engraved and the mechanism is the simple sear-lock type. The butt is a copy of the Catalan style popular on Spanish guns

Left:
This Viennese wheellock belonged to the Archbishop of Salzburg. It is dated 1568, and was made by Wolf Paumgartner. The mahogany stock has the early German butt form and is unusually plain, the decoration being concentrated on the metalwork. Iron pyrites, used to cause the sparks when held against the serrated wheel, has a soft crumbling composition, and for this reason many wheellocks were fitted with two dogs so that a spare pyrites would be immediately available

Facing page:
A superbly decorated wheel-lock rifle by Wenzel Böhm of Eger (in northwestern Bohemia) dating about 1775. The retention of the cheek-stock and large trigger guard is combined with rococo carving on the stock, gilt bronze mounts chiselled in typical mid-18th Century motifs, and the finely engraved lock with its large dog and concealed wheel, all features of later origin than the basic design

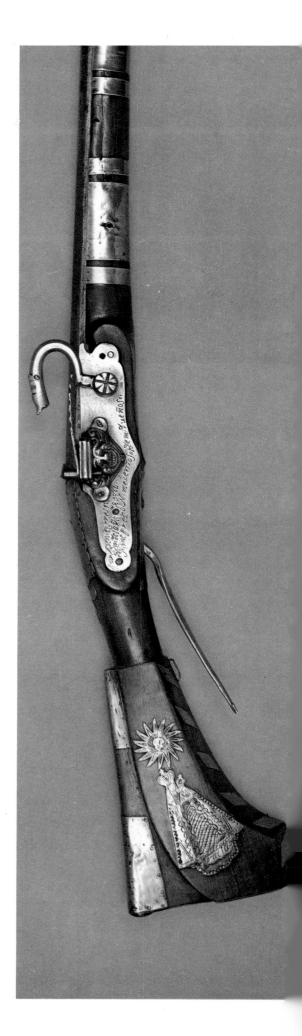

CHAPTER I

EARLY GUNS

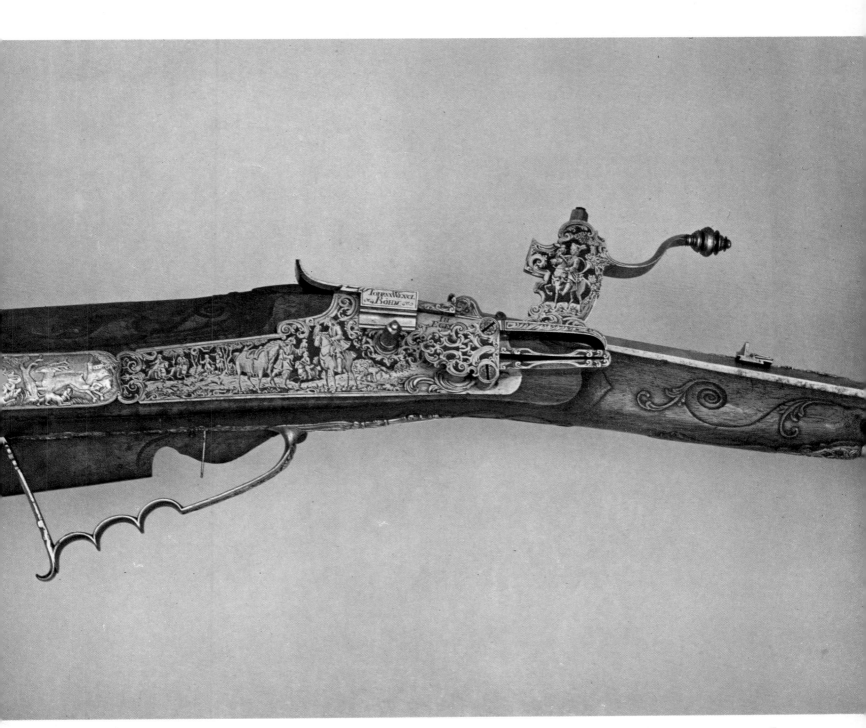

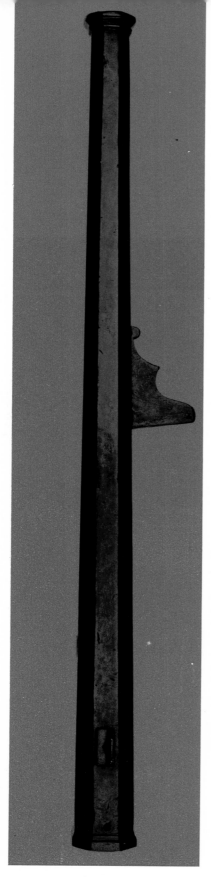

Despite the fact of its weighing 47 lb., being 38 – in. in length and having a one-inch bore, this bronze piece of probable French origin was known as a hand-gun! The description was to distinguish this type of weapon from cannon. This particular piece originally had a wooden tiller inserted into a recess or socket in the breech, and the block on the underside would have been rested on or against a wall for support and the taking-up of the recoil

Firearms, although usually considered in the light of highly anti-social instruments, have been far more influenced by social factors than many other mechanical devices. This is not merely because firearms lend themselves in varying degrees to decorative artistry or to the expression of mechanical ingenuity, but also because of the social attitude towards firearms throughout the centuries from their earliest development. It was not until they had been developed to the point of personal utility and mechanical reliability that firearms were widely accepted as objects worthy of careful attention and development, and not until they had been socially accepted was there any development of the skills and techniques of manufacture involved in producing firearms. For these reasons it is not until the Sixteenth Century that a serious study of firearms may be undertaken.

Firearms have always been a luxury item, even from the days when they were considered primarily as pyrotechnic devices; war being one of society's greatest luxuries, firearms naturally received early attention as objects well calculated to further the art of waging war. So long as bows and cross-bows, lances, spears and other edged weapons were in a preponderance there was no great impetus for the perfection of firearms, and it was several hundred years before they advanced beyond the stage of largely psychological phenomena whose noise and flame intimidated the enemy. Advancement in the skilled techniques of metallurgy was necessary before really effective projectile-firing weapons using an explosive substance could be produced. The development of firearms therefore depended largely upon the internal organisation and economic health of an area, and upon the degree of intelligent attention turned to the problem of producing them.

The beginnings. The discovery of what we now call gunpowder, as well as the first use of instruments designed for it, is shrouded in mystery because of a lack of documentation and confusion in the translation of what material is known. Original writers often used the same general terms to describe a variety of objects *one* of which might now be classified as a firearm. We do know that the use of incendiary materials was widespread during the 13th and 14th Centuries, and it is also known that in China a weak form of gunpowder was being used in the 11th Century although apparently not as a propellant charge.

The first reference to gunpowder being used as a propellant charge, again in China, occurs in 1130, in connexion with bamboo tubes. By 1259 a device called *hüo ch' iang* was firing solid fragments with a weak charge of gunpowder. The formula for gunpowder is thought to have been brought to Europe from China by Arab scholars, and the substance was referred to in European documents in the 1260s.

There are a great many legends regarding who first made guns in Europe. Almost every country has had the benefit of the scholarly 'discovery' of some native individual who made the very first guns, but in recent years most of these have been shown to be unfounded or downright spurious. Considering the dearth of contemporary evidence, it is far more reasonable to speak in terms of guns being in use by a certain decade, than to approach the question in terms of a certain date and place. Independent development in widely separated areas at about the same date is quite possible. In addition, there is no evidence to prove that the Chinese were producing metal guns before the Europeans.

The first date of real significance is 1326. In that year there were written and depicted several references to the manufacture and use of guns in England and in Italy, which clearly indicate that by this time the gun was a known and desirable object. We are speaking here of cannon; the first use of the term 'handgun' does not occur until 1388, but here again there is every reason to believe that smaller forms of guns were in existence, if not highly

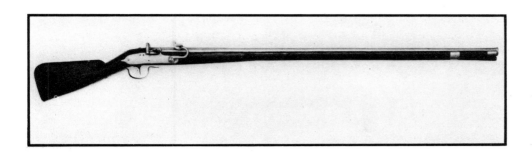

developed, at about the same time as the larger versions.

These 1326 references are of importance as the first concrete evidence of the European use of guns. The English materials include two manuscripts written by King Edward III's chaplain, Walter de Milemete, both of which illustrate cannon which are firing arrows. These are pot or vase-shaped guns of a type already in use in Italy and France. The manuscripts in question are *De Nobilitatibus, Sapientiis, et Prudentiis Regum* and *De Secretis Secretorum*. In Italy, the Council of Florence passed a decree authorising the appointment of two men to manufacture iron bullets or arrows, and metallic cannons for the castles and villages under its control. From the 1340s there are numerous references to the use of guns in the archives of most European countries, but this is all that can be said of these references, and we are left to judge the details by actual pieces which can be dated to this period.

During the course of the 14th Century handguns developed in three distinct forms, all of which have been identified in contemporary illustrations. These include cast bronze and wrought iron barrels which are bound to wooden stocks (sometimes referred to as 'tillers') by iron bands; iron and bronze barrels made with the exterior of the breech formed as a socket to receive a wooden shaft; and iron barrels with the breech section beaten out to form a long handle with a knob or a ring at the end. By the 1460s guns were

A German harquebus of about 1600, fitted with a snap-matchlock. The short fishtail or triangular butt and the long heavy barrel of this example, with the support on the underside of the fore-end, denote a fortress-defence gun. The arm has a 1-in. bore, the barrel being 69 in. long, and the weight 44 lb. 10 oz. The backsight is notched and also has an aperture

As a military longarm, the matchlock musket was finally withdrawn from service by all of the major powers of Europe only during the War of the Spanish Succession (1702-1713). By that date the flintlock had generally superseded the older forms except for militia and a variety of troops not associated with the usual definition of 'front-line troops'. This Anglo-Dutch musket of the reign of William III is typical of those in use during the last quarter of the 17th Century; the furniture is of thin sheet iron nailed to the stock, and the entire arm, with its .80 calibre 46 in. barrel, weighs 10 lb. 6 oz.

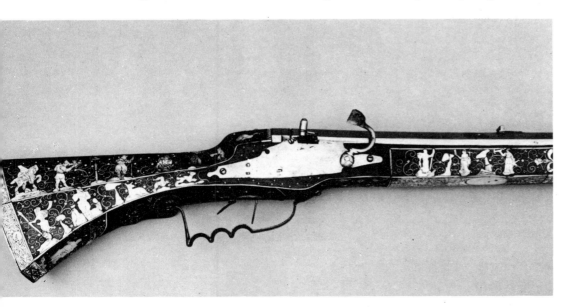

The absence of mechanical shock in the operation of the matchlock made it attractive for use on target-shooting weapons, just as later the wheel-lock was preferred to the flintlock such arms in Eastern Europe. This Swiss rifle is by B. von Reinach of Basle, and is dated 1619. The lockplate is of wheel-lock pattern and it appears that the rifle has been converted back to the matchlock system. It is fitted with a hair trigger. The .67 calibre barrel is 50 in. in length, and the rifle weighs 21 lb.

being fired from the shoulder, but this did not become common practice until the 17th Century when the straight or 'Spanish' butt came into wide use.

Until there was a definite need for an advance in the utility of the hand firearm no steps were taken to improve the hand-cannon. It was made with its breech and barrel as a solid mass, and ignited by holding a piece of lighted tinder, hot coal, or red-hot iron to the vent or touch-hole, which was bored on top of the breech. By the early part of the 15th Century, however, the techniques involved in manufacturing gunpowder had produced an improved product, and the effect – if not the efficiency – of firearms was correspondingly improved. During the early part of the 15th Century several major improvements were made in hand firearms tending towards the development of the familiar early musket.

The matchlock. The earliest recorded mechanical device for holding a match and bringing it into contact with a pan of priming powder has been traced back as far as 1411. This earliest form consisted of an 'S' or 'Z'-shaped hook pivoted in its centre, with one end acting as a match-holder and the other end as a trigger.

By the middle of the century further improvements had come into general use, including the fitting of a separate breech-plug which screwed into the breech of the barrel, and the fastening of the barrel to the full-length stock by the use of cross-pins passing through pierced tenons or loops brazed or dovetailed into the underside of the barrel. The introduction of a mechanical match-holding device also involved the drilling of the vent on the side of the barrel (normally the right side), and the fitting of a pan beneath it, often with a pan cover hinged over it which was swung to one side manually before firing.

The development of a mechanical device for igniting firearms naturally encouraged their use for military purposes, and during the 15th Century companies of infantry were armed with what came to be called arquebusses. The butt of these arms became more practical for firing from the shoulder, being flat and oblong, and named after the militia who used them – the *Landsknecht Kolbe*.

During the last quarter of the 15th Century two further improvements were made in the operation of the matchlock, forms which were to survive a very long time indeed in various parts of the world. The first of these was the snap matchlock, or *luntenschnappschloss*. There were a number of variations on the theme, but basically it consisted of a lockplate on the inside of which was a springed lever, pivoted laterally with a stud acting as a sear projecting through a hole in the lockplate. The match-holder is long, thin, and tubular in form, and has a projection at its base – called the toe if on the front, and the heel if on the rear – which catches on the sear projecting through the lockplate when the match-holder is raised. The match-holder (or serpentine, or cock) is released normally by pressing a button located either on the rear of the lockplate or in a recess on the wrist of the stock – the original button-trigger.

The second form of improved matchlock to appear in the latter part of the 15th Century was the one which was widely adopted for military arms for the next century. Its chief attributes were the simplicity of design and operation, and the cheapness of production, combined with a somewhat safer and more positive control of the lighted match. This mechanism consisted of a long sear lever pivoted vertically inside the lockplate under pressure of a mainspring. To one end of this was linked the serpentine or match-holder – generally on the front end of the lockplate on European examples – and on the other end was an extension lever which served as a trigger. The mainspring tension held the serpentine away from the pan,

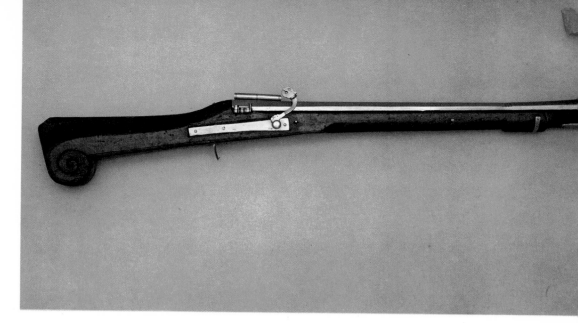

This very plain and simply constructed short matchlock is of the style called 'half harquebus' – with many variations in spelling – and is typical of the weapons supplied to mercenaries during the latter part of the 16th Century. The semi-rounded butt is associated with the earlier part of the century on German guns, but the snap-matchlock dates the arm later

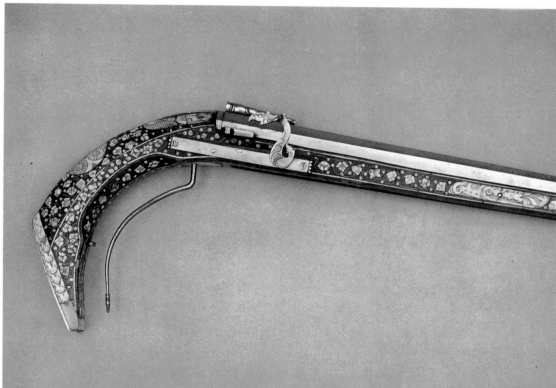

The extreme development of the petronel form of stock is shown in this French matchlock of about 1600. The sear-lock is typical, but the use of engraved bone inlay is somewhat unusual for French weapons, this material being more familiarly associated with Germanic weapons

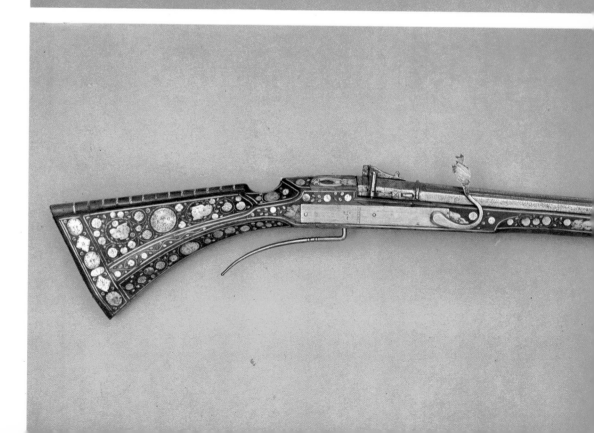

This German musket of about 1600 has a restrained form of the triangular or German musketeer's butt, and the stock is inlaid with delicately engraved mother of pearl and bone. The breech section of the barrel is fluted, and the mechanism is of the sear-lock type

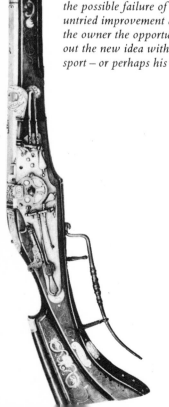

A very late survival of the matchlock, built on the lines of a flintlock, is this Flemish target gun by E. O. Siaens, about 1750. Double set triggers are fitted, and the butt has a cheekrest on each side. The aperture backsight originally had a hinged leaf. The gun has brass furniture, and a 42-in. barrel of .560 calibre. Of the several ignition systems used with muzzleloading firearms, the flintlock probably gave the most shock to the steady holding of the weapon, and the survival of both the matchlock and the wheellock for target arms is not therefore as unusual as it might seem

A combination matchlock-wheellock, dated 1603. This German arm has iron furniture, and a stock inlaid with staghorn decoration, and is fitted with trunnions for firing from a rest even though it weighs only 12 lb.
With each transition from one ignition system to another, weapons using both systems were made to guard against the possible failure of the new and untried improvement and also to give the owner the opportunity of trying out the new idea without sacrificing his sport – or perhaps his life

but pressure on the extension lever brought it downwards into the priming powder. This is the so-called 'sear-matchlock.'

From the beginning of the 16th Century the matchlock existed concurrently with other forms of ignition systems, principally the wheel-lock and then the snaphaunce. But because of its simplicity and cheapness the matchlock continued as the normal system used on military long-arms until it was superceded by the true flintlock during the last quarter of the 17th Century. There are as always, individual exceptions to this generalisation, but we are concerned here with the main trend of development. Various forms of sear and snap-matchlocks survived in normal use into the 19th Century, primarily in Japan, India, and China. In Europe the matchlock was occasionally used on locks of combination construction in company with a flintlock as late as the 1770s.

The final form of mechanical matchlock which may be considered as a part of the overall development of the system was the trigger-lock, or, as it was usually called at the time, the 'tricker-lock'. This improvement answered the need for a safer and more positive control over the serpentine, since the slightest pressure on the extension lever of the sear-matchlock was sufficient to bring the lighted match down into the priming. The lever of the sear-lock was replaced by the modern style of trigger, hung in a recess on the underside of the stock and protected by a strap of metal known as the trigger guard. The trigger was pivoted on a cross-pin through the stock, and it acted on the right-angle bend of the sear bar which was pivoted vertically on the inside of the lockplate. Although this obvious improvement was introduced during the last part of the 16th Century, the older form continued to be produced well into the 17th Century.

During the second half of the 17th Century the lockplate of the matchlock came to be shaped like that of the flintlock, and a further refinement was fitted to some locks in the form of a sliding pan-cover which moved aside automatically when the sear was pressed by the pulling of the trigger, thus uncovering the priming powder just before the match struck it.

Despite these several improvements the matchlock was still an awkward, unreliable, and slow weapon in use. The match had constantly to be attended to, and was almost impossible to keep lighted during wet or windy weather. The bayonet had not yet come into general use and firearms therefore formed a threat to an enemy only under ideal climatic conditions. The expedient usually adopted to render the matchlock more dependable was to keep both ends of the length of match alight, but there was really no satisfactory means of keeping an exposed spark in being.

Early classification. The 16th Century saw the real development and expansion of the gunmaking industry throughout Europe, and the organisation and classification of the various types of firearms in use, as well as the introduction of many new forms of weapon and ignition systems. This overall organisation reflected the social order gradually developing in Europe, along with the aspirations of the various dynasties to acquire pre-eminence in one quarter or another. The affluence of the nobility and their

The wheel-lock was 'cocked' by winding-up the wheel with a spanner which fitted over the square axle in the centre of the wheel. This was connected by a short chain to the mainspring. The 'dog' or pyrites holder was lowered onto the pan manually and held in position by the spring beneath it. When the trigger was pulled the wheel revolved against the pyrites and sparks were instantly created which ignited the priming in the pan.

increasing level of knowledge was reflected in the interest now taken in decorated firearms, and it is from this source that a major portion of firearms production owed its origins until the 19th Century. The interest and the money put forward by the upper classes formed the basis for the mechanical and artistic developments in both sporting and military firearms throughout Europe.

The earliest term applied generically to all forms of handguns was *arquebus*, also rendered in a number of variations including harquebus, hackbut, or hagbut; the term was used for all types of portable firearms during the first half of the 16th Century, while at the same time wall guns (which were generally enlarged versions of current longarms made to be fired from the walls of fortresses) were referred to as *arquebusses a croc*. Smaller arms, corresponding roughly to the later carbine, were termed *half hagis* or *demihakes*.

During the last half of the 16th Century several new names for firearms appeared, including musket, basterd musket, and petronel. The caliver also appears, as a somewhat later replacement for the basterd musket. The largest of this group was the *musket*, which was large enough to need the aid of a forked rest when fired – a form described as early as 1499.

These muskets were fully stocked weapons, directly descendant from the earlier arquebus, but apparently heavier. At this period two types of stock were common on muskets: the straight, or Spanish stock, which was intended to be fired from the shoulder, and the crooked, or French stock, which was to be fired from the chest. It is interesting to note that muskets were still being used to fire arrows as well as ball, a practice which continued in England at least until 1588, with references to their use as late as 1693.

In the last quarter of the 16th Century the English musket was described as having a standard barrel length of four feet, carrying twelve balls to the pound of lead (or 12 gauge, the actual bore size varying from 10 to 11 gauge). The *basterd musket* was merely a shorter-barrelled version of the same bore size. The *petronel* was developed from earlier French stocked guns of larger size, but because of the weight and recoil the petronel was normally made as a light carbine for mounted use, and in time came to be applied to all forms of cavalry or light sporting carbines intended to be used from horse-back, regardless of stock pattern. These came into being during the third quarter of the 16th Century, and were normally fitted with wheel-locks.

Innovations in mechanical design are to be found as far back as mechanisms were applied to the ignition of firearms. This north German carbine of about 1580 is built with a completely enclosed lock; the wheel being cocked or spanned through a hole in the left side of the stock. The wheel cover bears the coat of arms of the city of Stettin, and the stock is inlaid with staghorn. The .41 calibre barrel is only 24 in. in length

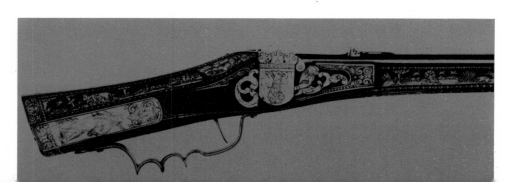

13

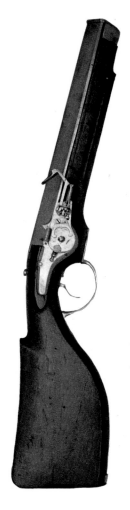

Contemporary writers on firearms differ considerably in their definitions of particular types, which makes any understanding of current attitudes and tactical concepts difficult, but we are fortunate in having an English tabulation dated 1630, which at least for that country brings some order out of chaos. The standard sizes for military longarms in England at this date were laid down as:

Musket	4 ft barrel	5 ft 2 in. overall	12 gauge
Caliver	3 ft.3 in.	4 ft 6 in. overall	17 gauge
Harquebus	2 ft 6 in.	3 ft overall	17 gauge
Carbine			
or			
Petronel	2 ft 6 in.	3 ft overall	24 gauge

The wheel-lock. Although the credit for the original idea of a wheel-lock mechanism may with reason be given to Leonardo da Vinci, *c.* 1500, and the earliest wheel-locks are of Italian construction, it is beyond question that the Germans were primarily responsible for the development of the mechanism and for the overwhelming majority of its production. It is for this reason that the positive identification of unmarked firearms dating from the 16th and early 17th Centuries is so difficult; not only did the Germans produce the largest number of wheel-lock arms, but they developed a thriving export trade in the locks alone, and in barrels. The arms-making centres of Augsburg and Nuremberg were the largest producers of wheel-locks. The earliest dated wheel-lock (1530) came from Augsburg.

The introduction of the wheel-lock as an ignition system for firearms caused a basic change in the attitude towards firearms, and brought about their acceptance and then encouragement for non-military purposes. In addition, the new system made practical the design and wide use of the first true pistol. The wheel-lock possessed several features of primary importance to the sportsman, when compared to the matchlock:

1. Once primed and spanned, with the dog lying against the pan-cover it was ready to fire instantly by simply pulling the trigger.
2. It was far less susceptible to weather conditions, either damp or wind,

'There is nothing new under the sun' aptly labels this German wheel-lock carbine of about 1620 – made to fire 22 shots simultaneously from five barrels, using superimposed charges. This same design was later employed on flintlocks probably made in the same region

This tschinke dating from about 1620 is unusual for the quantity and ornateness of its decoration. The barrel is overlaid with engraved brass, and the lock has been given similar treatment. The stock is inlaid with engraved brass and engraved bone, the latter in some cases being stained green. Although ornate, the quality of the work is not superior to that found on the majority of tschinkes

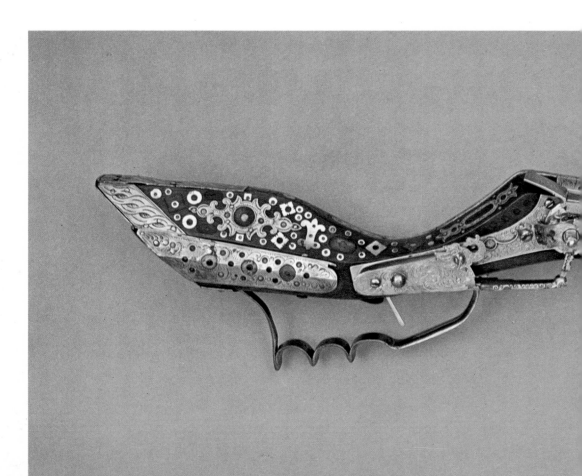

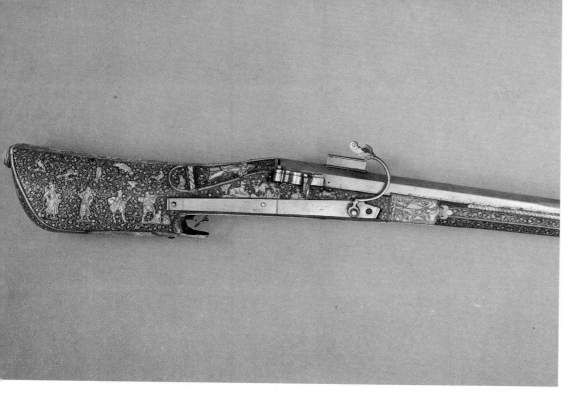

This exquisite Bohemian matchlock target gun is dated 1584, and was made in the town of Mergenthal. The stock, on which the underside is formed to act partially as a trigger guard, is profusely inlaid with bone and larger plaques of ivory, finely engraved. The gun is made without a ramrod in the manner of many target weapons until the end of muzzle-loaders. This particular style of cheekstock is associated with northern European arms of the 16th Century

since there was no open spark, and the priming pan was covered until the instant of firing.

3. Firing, once the trigger was pulled, was virtually instantaneous, even quicker than the later flintlock.

4. It could be carried loaded, primed and ready to fire in any position, e.g. in saddle holsters, on a sling over the shoulder, etc., thereby making it thoroughly practical for mounted use either for military or sporting purposes.

This form of firearm, therefore, could challenge the virtues of the bow, crossbow, or spear in the hunting field, and offer a new and highly effective weapon for cavalry. Although not true in the strictest sense of the term, since a few decorated matchlocks were made, it may be generally accepted that the advent of the wheel-lock heralded the entry of the highly decorated firearm upon the stage of history, and made of firearms generally an object worthy of embellishment, and one worthy of presentation to princes and kings as a token of esteem.

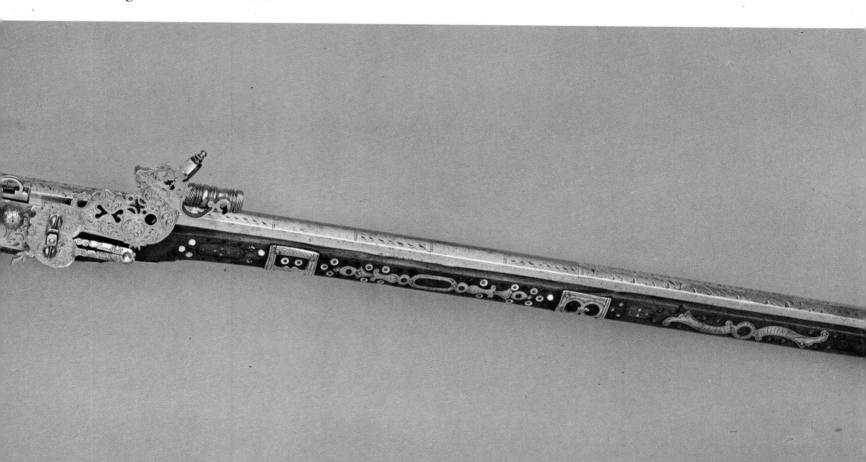

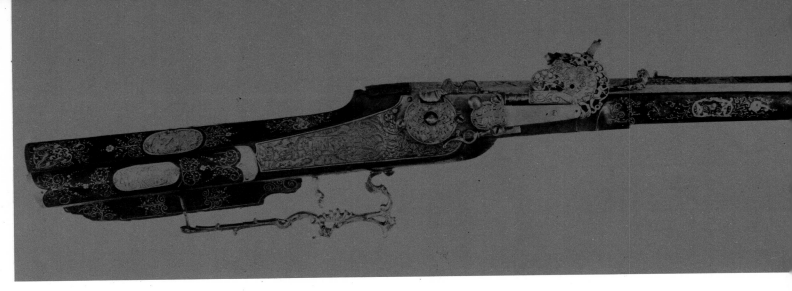

*This high quality Polish rifle is in
marked contrast to the tschinke
although coming from the same general
area at about this same time (this rifle
dates from about 1640). The cheekstock
has silver wire inlay and pierced silver
plaques backed by gilt copper.
The trigger guard is of gilt bronze.
The lockplate is engraved with a
mounted combat scene. The barrel is
39 in. long, and the bore .425 calibre,
rifled with eight grooves
Below: As the petronel was associated
with western European light sporting
arms, so the tschinke is typical of
eastern Europe. Made in and around
Teschen on the frontiers of Bohemia
and Saxony, they were intended as
small lightweight birding guns, seem
to have been made in large numbers,
and are generally not of as good
quality as other wheellock arms.
The large external mainspring
and mere bracket covering the wheel
are normal features, as is the shape of
the cheekstock, and the crude
mother-of-pearl and staghorn inlays.
This example dates from about 1620,
has a 37– in. barrel of .300 calibre,
and weighs only 5 lb. 10 oz.*

However, because of its complicated, costly, and fragile mechanism, the wheel-lock was confined very largely to sporting and presentation arms, and was little used for military weapons with the single and notable exception of cavalry pistols. Pistols are first recorded in the hands of troopers in Germany in the 1540s, and are common from that time until the 1660s, when the flintlock supplanted them. These cavalry pistols were very plain, and generally slender in outline, and were apparently reserved for special units of the better sort, even though cavalry at this period was normally composed of superior quality personnel, many of whom supplied their own arms.

The use of pistols by mounted troops brought immediate tactical, and basic strategic changes in the use of this arm of the service. In addition there were some wheel-lock carbines made for cavalry, but these were in very limited use compared with pistols, and were very largely confined to sporting petronels. It may be noted here that pistols were commonly used for sporting purposes from the introduction of the wheel-lock early in the 16th Century, until the close of the 18th Century, particularly in central and eastern Europe, which goes far to explain the large numbers of superbly decorated pairs of wheel-lock, snaphaunce, and flintlock pistols made during these years.

As indicated earlier, the wheel-lock was largely an international product manufactured, and apparently largely assembled into complete weapons as well, in Germany, and exported throughout Europe. There were a few 'local' features which crept into the design of the wheel-lock, particularly in the earlier years, in Northern Italy and especially in France. French

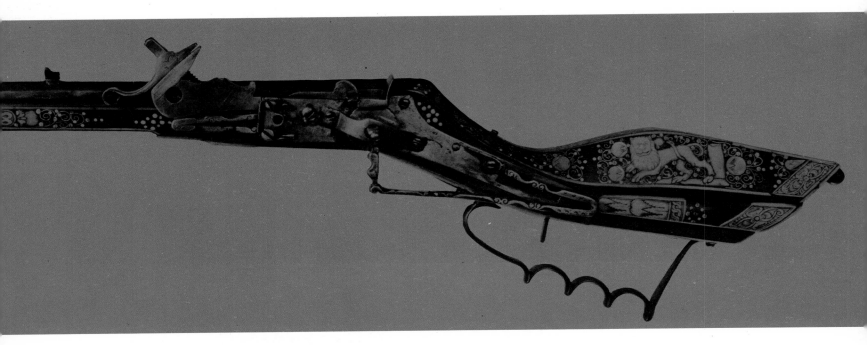

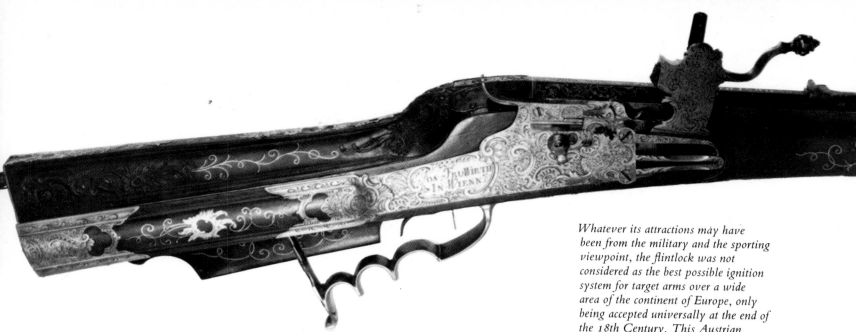

Whatever its attractions may have been from the military and the sporting viewpoint, the flintlock was not considered as the best possible ignition system for target arms over a wide area of the continent of Europe, only being accepted universally at the end of the 18th Century. This Austrian target rifle with its internal wheel and rococo scrollwork dates from about 1740, and is by the famed Joseph Fruwirth of Vienna. The weight of the barrel and the light charge used made use of the shoulder stock unnecessary, consequently the cheekstock was retained on these late wheellock rifles

wheel-locks feature a spindle extending all the way across the stock, which is spanned from the left side and not the right. Italian wheel-locks often have a spare dog, or pyrites holder, fitted. But to speak of 'national characteristics' in the wheel-lock, even as regards decoration, would be, if not entirely inaccurate, certainly misleading in the sense that this term may only justifiably be applied to the flintlock.

Wheel-locks are overwhelmingly 'German' in their design, construction, and decoration, as regards the main stream of the evolution of firearms. It is important to remember, at this point, that the wheel-lock was a mechanism limited in its application by its costliness, fragility and intricate construction, and that both the older matchlock and newer forms of ignition were in use during almost the entire period covered by its use in sporting and other high quality arms. As a commentary on the attitude towards even the superior efficiency of the wheel-lock, it is interesting to note that all of the earliest-known wheel-locks form parts of combination weapons, and are found combined with cross-bows, axes, swords and daggers, and war hammers.

The rifled barrel. As with the 'invention' of gunpowder and the first firearms, there is a multitude of legends and stories surrounding the invention of the rifled barrel, and the causes for the invention, all of which have been exploded as 'not proven' by research in recent years. It is generally accepted that the rifled barrel is of German origin, probably south German, and that while it may have made its appearance during the first quarter of the 16th Century, it was not generally known even in southern Germany until the 1550s.

It is thought that the initial discovery was connected with a means of reducing the effects of fouling, and facilitating loading by cutting grooves in the surface of the bore which could collect fouling. Wrapping the ball in a patch of thin leather or cloth did not come in at the same time as the rifled barrel, but is again considered to be a German innovation which occurred in the 17th Century.

It may be that the earliest rifles had *straight rifling*, the grooves being made parallel with the bore and without any inclination or twist. This was a form which survived with normal rifling, and was in use as late as the 1860s, having over the years been adopted for military purposes by various European countries as a compromise between the smooth-bore and the spirally-rifled bore which created loading difficulties.

All of the important forms of rifling which, during the 19th Century were 'discovered' to possess unique qualities of accuracy or tendencies not to foul, were in use during the 16th or 17th Centuries, including the oval bore, hexagonal bore, ratchet rifling, gaining twist rifling, and progressive

Right: as with later arms, the plain examples have a much poorer survival rate than the highly decorated pieces. This Tyrolean rifle by Andreas Brantner is dated 1672, and may well have been a game-keeper's or forester's rifle. The lock has an internal wheel. The stock has a staghorn fore-end cap, and the fore-end is fluted, but aside from some elementary border carving the weapon is quite plain, and robustly built

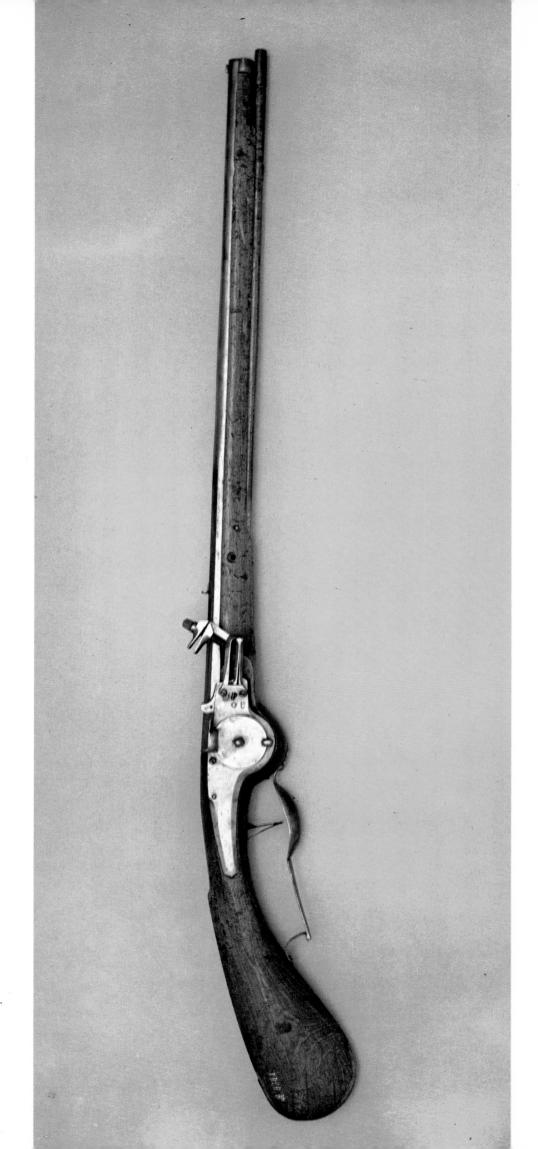

The paddle-shaped butt was a feature
of northern European stock design
during the second and third quarters of
the 17th Century. This German
wheel-lock carbine, intended for
cavalry use, dates about 1650

18

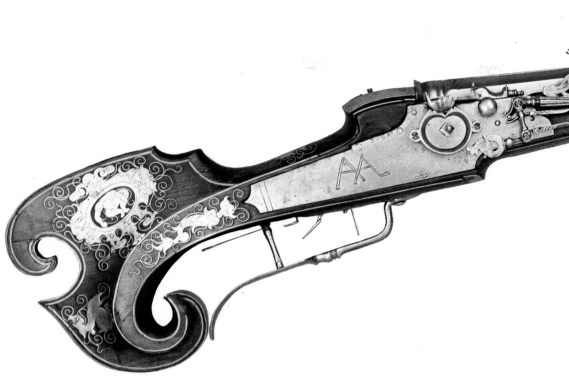

This wheel-lock musket was made in Strassbourg at the end of the 16th Century, and comes from the gewehrkammer of Count Thun of Tetschen. The walnut stock has brass inlay work, and the peculiar shape of the stock is termed the snail-ended butt

North German wheellock rifle dated 1687, with a French-style shoulder butt of very early form. The Germanic adaptation of the French pattern then becoming popular in much of Europe includes the use of a sliding wooden covered butt-trap, and the steel wire and nail inlay work, as well as the large trigger guard with finger grips

depth rifling. There were also some forms which did not, for obvious reasons, survive, such as the square and diamond and triangular-shaped bore. During the 18th Century several German makers produced a literally heart-shaped bore, with the exterior form of the barrel (and ramrod) to match.

The difficulties of loading a rifled barrel – even when the naked ball was not beaten down the length of the bore with the aid of a mallet, but was encased in a bit of greased leather or cloth – made it wholly impractical as a military weapon, but its use by small groups of temporarily raised marksmen was nevertheless usual from the 17th Century. The first organised use of a body of riflemen may be credited to William of Hesse who raised such a corps in 1631. The first permanently established rifle corps was raised by Frederick II (the Great) of Prussia in 1740, and expanded in 1744. By the time of the Seven Years War (1756-63) most of the countries engaged had riflemen in their service on a regular basis. The first permanent British rifle corps was not raised until 1800, although small unites of Continental riflemen had performed their functions during the Seven Years, American, and French Revolutionary Wars, in the service of the British Crown.

In connexion with the difficulties of loading a rifled barrel, it may be mentioned that breech-loading was early adopted as one means of circumventing this problem, but that it never met with a great deal of success due to the inability to produce mechanically near-perfect fitting surfaces which would function properly given the 'dirty' properties of gunpowder. The English seem to have preferred breech-loading types for their rifles, and did not 'revert' to the muzzle loading type generally until the last quarter of the 18th Century. Breech-loaders, while they encompass a fascinating field of study for students of early firearms, do not come into any discussion of the maintream of development of firearms, as they were distinctly a curiosity at the time, along with various ingenious types of repeating weapons.

The use of the rifle was very largely restricted to central and southern Germany, the Scandinavian countries, and Russia from the 16th through to the 18th Century. Its introduction into the British North American colonies during the second quarter of the 18th Century created far more psychological than practical effects which have been greatly exaggerated by national historians. A detailed study of the development of the rifle is a fascinating and often humourous undertaking, but it should be clearly borne in mind that in terms of the development of firearms generally, the

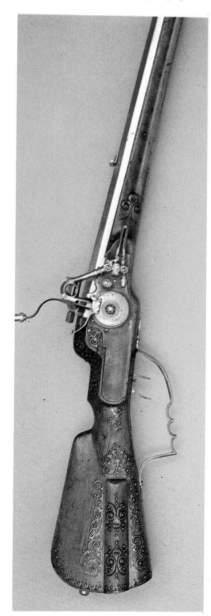

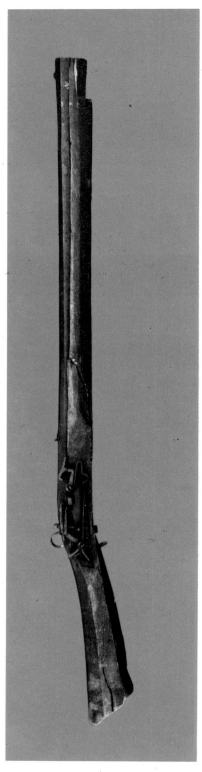

The Scandinavian or Baltic lock was one of the regional variations of the snaphaunce, and was subsequently modernised into a flintlock.
The peculiar form of the cock, the swivelling steel, and manually operated pan cover are typical features. This Finnish rifle dating from the early 18th Century has a German cheekstock which has been elongated for firing from the shoulder. No trigger guard was provided. The rifle weighs 14 lb., and has a 31 in. barrel of .525 calibre

rifle takes a definite second place in favour of the sporting gun, military longarms, and pistols until the 19th Century when reasons for its development and expanded acceptance come into being both in the social, economic, and technological fields.

One form of rifle peculiar to the wheel-lock ignition system, a lightweight piece developed and made largely in the area centred on Teschen, was called the *tschinke*. This was designed to be used for shooting sitting birds, and was produced in large numbers during the years from the middle of the 16th Century. The mainspring of the tschinke lock was external, the bores were small in size compared with other contemporary sporting rifles, and the inlaid stag-horn and mother-of-pearl decoration of the stocks was lavish but not well finished as a general rule. This type of 'birding rifle' was produced until the latter part of the 17th Century, by which time shooting birds on the wing had become accepted as the preferred method of pursuing this form of sport.

Rifling was not generally applied to pistols until the 19th Century, with the consipicuous exception of English 'turn-off' pistols made from the middle of the 17th Century. In these pistols the barrel screwed-off from the breech just ahead of the chamber section, which was then breech loaded. The ball was slightly over bore size and offered an ideal opportunity for the use of rifling. But even with this ideal form, rifling in the 'turn-off' pistol was usually omitted after the beginning of the 18th Century. Some rifled carbines were also made in England during the last half of the 17th Century on this system.

The wheel-lock rifle generally follows the Germanic form, with its 'cheek-stock' and heavy octogonal barrel, inlaid full-length stock, and lavishly chiselled or engraved mounts. Because of its speed of ignition and reliability, the wheel-lock continued to be used by some German and Austrian makers for target rifles until the beginning of the 19th Century, and on sporting rifles down to the middle of the 18th Century. Later wheel-locks are considerably streamlined when compared to the earlier types. The wheel, arm of the dog, and the dog-spring were placed inside the lockplate. In addition, later locks often had a self-spanning device actuated by the moving of the dog into the firing position.

The snaphaunce. As has been observed earlier, the wheel-lock was a complicated, delicate, and expensive mechanism to produce, and was not therefore practical for the general run of weapons. It is not surprising that other methods of ignition were sought, and soon devised. What may be accepted as the earliest form of the flintlock appeared in Sweden in 1539, but there is some question whether this did not originate from Germany. It should be understood that the term 'snaphaunce' is a later derivation, and that all forms of this and the later true, or 'French flintlock', were originally called flintlocks. However, in deference to common usage, the term 'snaphaunce' will be used here to describe those forms of the flintlock in which the steel is separate from the pan cover (regardless of the construction of the sear), and the term 'flintlock' will be applied to those having the pan cover and the steel combined into one 'L'-shaped piece, again regardless of the construction of the sear. A snaphaunce mechanism appeared in Florence in 1547, and the earliest complete weapon known at present was set up in Sweden in 1556 with a lock bearing a Nuremberg mark, again pointing to the German origins of the snaphaunce lock.

The Baltic or Scandanavian lock is the earliest production form of the snaphaunce, and continued to be used in the countries surrounding the Baltic Sea for some two hundred years. It is also the first of those mechanisms which may be considered as 'ethnic' or 'national', and continued to be preferred in a particular geographic region long after it had been replaced by an improved design in other areas. The Italian snaphaunce, Spanish miquelet, Englishlock, and Roman-lock all fall into this category.

The earliest pattern of Baltic lock has an external mainspring, but this was removed to the inside of the plate during the 17th Century. In this type of snaphaunce the sear is pivoted horizontally and passes through the lock-plate just in rear of the cock, bearing upon the tail of the cock. The front of the cock, or toe, is borne upon by the rear of the mainspring, and later this arrangement is replaced by the spring bearing upon an internal tumbler. The pan cover is moved manually to one side before firing. The jaws of the cock are long and narrow, and the cock itself is usually rounded in form and made in a long curve. From the second half of the 17th Century the steel and pan cover are hinged together, so that the steel may be turned to one side to render the lock 'safe' while the pan remains covered. Later examples also have notches cut into the tumbler which engage the sear rather than the tail of the cock.

The snaphaunce came to France during the third quarter of the 16th Century, and is first mentioned in England in 1580. The earliest German production snaphaunces are military arms combining a matchlock mechanism, and date from the 1570s. In Northern Italy the wheel-lock was not ousted until the early part of the 17th Century, while in southern Italy the trend closely followed Spanish progress with an entirely different type of lock from that which was prominent in the northern section of the country. The northern Italians adopted the French, or vertical, sear but retained the separate steel and pan cover as presenting more surface for artistic embellishment. The southern Italians adopted the horizontally acting sear and an external mainspring, but with the steel and pan cover combined as one – a true flintlock.

The normal early form of European snaphaunce has a horizontally acting sear which engages the tail, or heel, of the cock directly, without a tumbler. The pan cover is manually operated until an automatically opening system was developed in the Low Countries during the last quarter of the 16th Century, which was widely copied and exported.

Despite this listing of 'first appearances' it must be stressed that the snaphaunce did not replace either the wheel-lock or the matchlock until the middle of the 17th Century in some areas, and that it may be considered as a transition system which was hardly established before being in its turn replaced by the true French flintlock. It retained its popularity in northern Italy until the early 19th Century, but in other areas the combining of the steel and pan cover, and the use of the vertically acting sear early recommended themselves as considerable improvements, and created what we now accept as the true flintlock, during the first half of the 17th Century.

The snaphaunce lock early developed into several regional variations across the continent of Europe, this example being a central Italian version of about 1750. The principal feature which distinguishes it from the true flintlock is the separation into two parts of the steel and the pan cover. Most sporting snaphaunces have pan covers automatically removed by the action of the tumble or other internal arrangements. Both snaphaunce and flintlock were produced concurrently in many Continental countries during the 17th and first half of the 18th Centuries

CHAPTER II
FLINTLOCK AND PERCUSSION GUNS

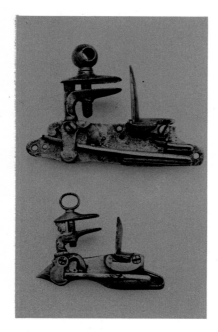

The Spanish miquelet lock is mechanically an early form of the true flintlock, differing in operation from the French lock in having a horizontally-acting sear which bears directly on the cock through the lockplate. The upper lock is a Spanish military Model 1802 Musket, and the lower is a Neapolitan pistol lock, circa 1780. The external mounting of the lock mechanism continued to be popular in the Mediterranean countries until the breech-loading era

An English-lock musket circa 1620. This is probably a conversion from matchlock, and is typical of the early 17th Century military musket in its general outline. The decoration of staghorn and mother of pearl indicate private ownership, and superior quality to King's arms. The 50-in. barrel is .75 calibre, and the musket weighs 12 lb. 10 oz.

The beginning of the 17th Century witnessed the introduction of two forms of gun-lock which were to dominate production in their respective areas for the next two hundred and twenty five years: the Spanish (or 'Mediterranean' or 'miquelet') lock, and the true or 'French' flintlock. They made their appearance at about the same time, although the 'invention' of the French lock may be dated with a little more certainty than the development of the miquelet. As it was developed from the earlier Italian snap-lock, the miquelet may be slightly earlier, but the French lock is now generally accepted as having been first produced by a gunmaker of Lisieux, Marin le Bourgeoys, sometime between 1600 and 1610.

It was not until the decade of the 1640s that either style began to be used in preference to other types of ignition systems already in use such as the wheel-lock and snaphaunce. It was only as the result of the virtual hegemony of France on the Continent beginning in the second half of the 17th Century that the 'French' flintlock eventually ousted most of its rivals, for of these there were many, all developed in certain areas and quite justifiably classed as 'nationalistic' expressions within the field of gun-making.

Locks included in this group of variations on the flintlock or snaphaunce are the English lock, Spanish and Italian forms of the miquelet, the Scandinavian lock, and the Madrid lock. It is significant that these mechanisms enjoyed popularity outside areas of strong French influence. There is little doubt that the survival of these several patterns was due in part to a conscious reaction against the overwhelming French influence in all artistic expression from the latter part of the 17th Century until the latter part of the 18th Century. With the exception of the English lock, all of these forms enjoyed a lengthy popularity in their respective areas, and indeed the miquelet lock was never entirely replaced by other forms prior to the introduction of the percussion system in Spain.

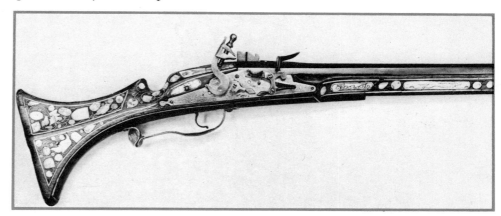

The English lock made its appearance during the first quarter of the 17th Century, and was almost entirely superceded by the French lock by the time of the Restoration of Charles II in 1660. Its main features included the combining of the firing mechanism of the snaphaunce lock with a steel and pan-cover now formed as one piece, as on the French lock. The sear operated horizontally through the lockplate on early examples, and on later ones engaged half- and full-cock notches on the tumbler, but still horizontally. As there was no shoulder on the inside of the cock, a stop was normally screwed to the outside of the lockplate which was struck by the breast of the cock. The separate sliding pan cover and the link to the tumbler which operated it were accordingly dispensed with.

An additional safety device was fitted on later examples which is commonly known as the *dog-catch*, and locks therewith supplied as *dog-locks*. This was simply a hook screwed to the lockplate in rear of the cock, which engaged in a notch cut on the back of the cock when it was raised about half-way, or slightly above the half-cock notch. When engaged, the piece could

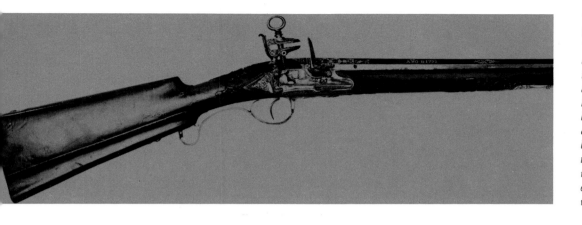

This Spanish lady's gun by Bustindui is mounted in silver, and is dated 1792. The lock is the usual miquelet type, and the shape of the butt is known as the 'Madrid stock'. The lock is chiselled and gilt, and the blued barrel has gold decoration. The 30-in. barrel is 21 bore, and the gun weighs only 3 lb. 13 oz. The use of longarms by European ladies was far greater than is generally realised, and many weapons built on a reduced scale erroneously described as 'boy's guns' were in fact made for feminine shooters

Firearms and edged weapons as arms for mounted troops each enjoyed periodic vogues until quite recent times when the breech-loading metallic cartridge firearm finally ousted other weapons. As with most late 17th Century military arms, this English cavalry carbine of the reign of James II, by Pickford, closely followed French patterns.
A long bar on the left side allowed the carbine to be carried on a shoulder sling, the butt resting in a bucket on the saddle. This example has a brass buttplate and ramrod pipes, and a sheet iron guard. The 31 in. barrel is .66 calibre

Target shooting has always been a specialised sport demanding suitably precise apparatus, as evidenced by this French target rifle of about 1675 by Les Soissons of Grenoble.
Features which continued to appeal to the target shooter are the full pistol grip, the aperture backsight – in this case a tubular one – and the relatively small bore, .635 calibre, as well as a separate loading rod. The carved ebony stock has chiselled steel mounts. The rounded form of the lock was a standard design for French weapons in the 17th and for most of the first half of the 18th Century

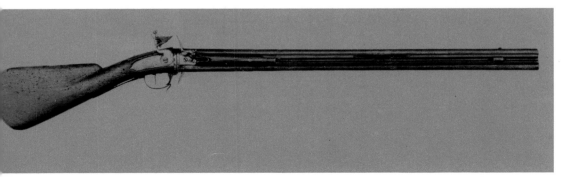

Double-barrelled arms were generally made in the superposed or over-under style until the side-by-side design began gaining in popularity from the middle of the 18th Century.
The swivel-breech or wender system, as shown on this Dutch 20 bore gun of circa 1685, made for a more compact arm as only one lock was necessary, but the pivoting mechanisms were often weakly made and easily worked loose

25

The idea of rotating barrels was hardly a new one when this double rifle was made in Munich about 1855. The use of a Swiss pattern backsight is unusual, but generally the decorative features including the style of stock carving and the use of a horn grip behind the trigger guard bow, as well as the engraving and chiselling of the metal parts, are typical of German sporting arms of the late percussion and early breech-loading era

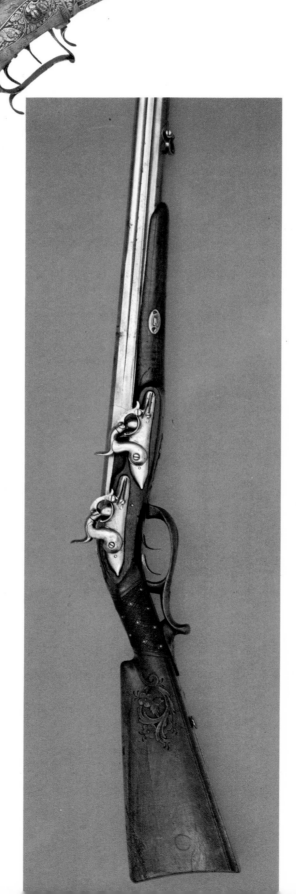

A German percussion combination gun and rifle or bockgewehr of about 1835. The unusual arrangement of the locks and consequent alterations in stock design seems to have found favour with some French and Belgian makers. The cap-holders on the locks were a popular device on early percussion weapons all over Germany, several military weapons being fitted with them until practice proved them an un-necessary refinement. The wooden trigger guard is re-inforced with a brass strip

This 19th Century Bosnian rifle shows few basic changes from its 18th Cntury Turkish predecessor. The lock and barrel are inlaid with silver, the barrel bands are hammered silver, and the style of the decoration although understandably Turkish in its origins, is peculiarly Bosnian in design

26

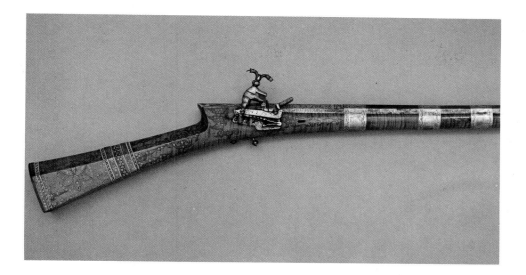

not be fired until the cock was drawn back to full-cock, when the dog moved back out of the notch in the cock. This dog-catch enjoyed short periods of popularity in several counties, but continued as a standard feature on Swedish military locks until the 1850s.

In the Spanish form of the miquelet lock, which was by far the most widely used and produced, the mechanism is primarily on the outside of the lock-plate, which means that very little wood need be removed to fit such a lock, giving the small of the stock far greater strength. The mainspring presses upwards against the rear portion or heel of the cock. Both arms of the horizontally-acting sear come through the lockplate in front of the cock, and the breast of the cock is formed with a stud to engage the halfcock arm, and as a blade to catch the full-cock arm. When the trigger is pressed, both arms of the sear are drawn back to allow the cock to fall. The steel and pan-cover are combined as on the true flintlock.

The Italian lock also has most of the mechanism mounted externally, but generally on a lockplate more in the French style. In the Italian lock, however, the arms of the sear come through the lockplate one at the rear or heel of the cock, and the other at the lower front or toe of the cock. The cock is so formed as to engage these studs of the sear, the front arm acting as half-cock, and the rear as full-cock. As on the Spanish lock, the hook of the mainspring engages the cock directly, but on the Italian version it presses downward on the front of the cock. Both the Spanish and Italian forms of the miquelet normally have the large ring-head jaw screw.

The Scandinavian lock developed directly from the snaphaunce during the 16th Century, but went through several variations in design which eventually included the use of a full-cock notch in place of the sear acting through the lockplate on the heel of the cock, and the screwing together of the steel and pan cover in such a way that not only are they combined into one piece, but that the steel may be swung to one side, thus rendering the lock safe without the need of a half-cock notch. The Scandinavian lock remained in use in the Baltic regions until the middle of the 18th Century when it was largely superseded by variations on the French form of lock – which pattern had already been in use on military arms since the end of the 17th Century.

The Madrid lock was an expression of French influence in a Spanish idiom. Its non-ethnic status is reinforced by the fact it was used only on arms for the elite, after the accession of Louis XIV's grandson as Philip V in 1701. Its use on fine quality weapons continued through the 18th Century. It may be described as a French lock in overall design, except that the sear still operates through the lockplate to engage, in the Italian manner, steps in the breast of the cock for half-cock, and on the heel for full-cock. These steps are generally quite unobstrusive. The large ring-head jaw screw is retained.

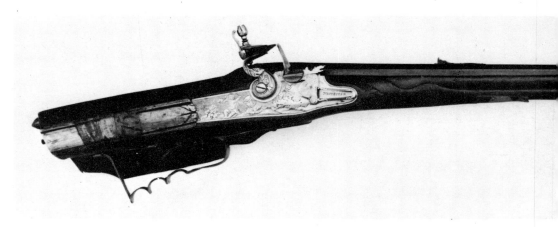

The French flintlock. Finally we come to the 'standard', 'true', or 'French flintlock' which, due to political and social as well as mechanical considerations was eventually to supersede all other forms with the exception of the miquelet. Its significant mechanical features include a vertically-acting sear which engaged in half and full-cock notches in the tumbler; and the one-piece combined steel and pan-cover, which was contemporarily known as the hammer, or more recently, the frizzen, battery, or steel. This lock came into use early in the 17th Century in France, but was not in general use until the 1630s and 40s. The adoption of it by the French army in the 1670s led to its spread throughout central and northern Europe by the end of the century, and by the time of the War of the Spanish Succession (1701-13) it came into almost universal use on military arms, as well as general use with the exceptions previously described.

The 17th Century was a war-torn era requiring vast quantities of cheap military weapons over a long span of years. For this reason the matchlock survived far longer than might otherwise have been the case, and there are some instances of its use by troops during the War of the Spanish Succession. The use of the wheel-lock for cavalry pistols was quickly superceded by the flintlock. It was largely due to the tremendous strain placed upon the manufacturing facilities of the antagonists during these war years that the system of great national armouries grew up during the relative peace of the second quarter of the 18th Century. The entire logistic structure of the emerging nation-states was reformed to provide a larger number of reasonably uniform weapons and equipment.

The enormous influence of French design and taste which spread more or less rapidly over the Continent from the early 1660s did not reach England in force until after the revocation of the Edict of Nantes, in 1685, after which date the emigration of large numbers of Huguenot gun-makers from France caused French influence to replace Dutch, which had been the predominant guide since the Restoration in 1660. From this time the overall design and decoration of English personal weapons, as opposed to military, closely followed French patterns, generally a decade or so behind the originals.

Even so, there were a number of features peculiarly English about the firearms produced during the period of French influence from about 1690 through the reign of George II. Amongst the most prominent of these were

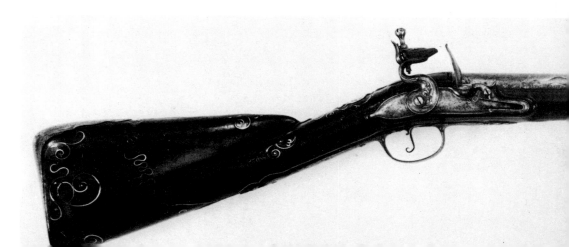

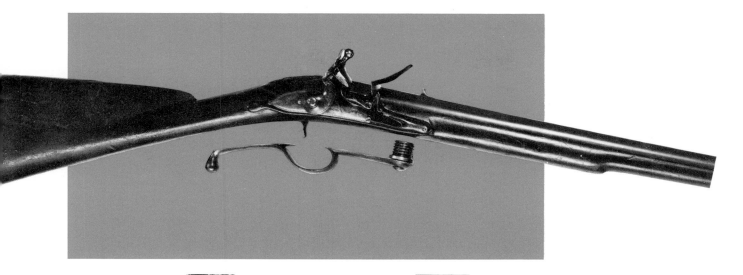

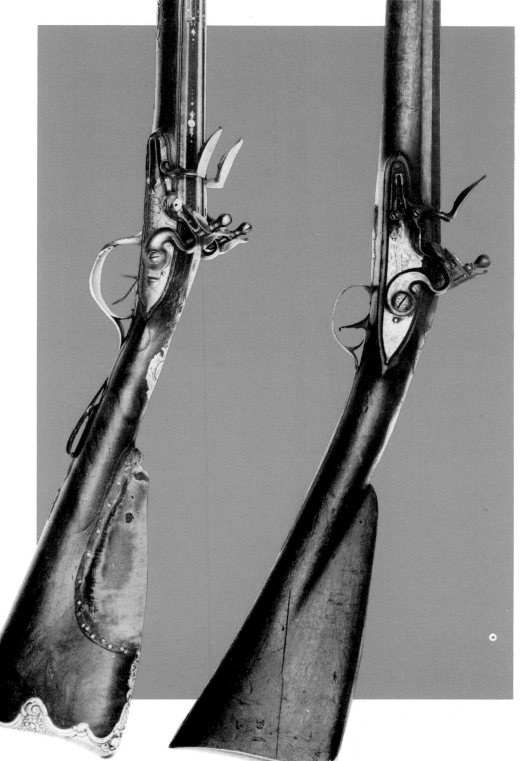

The English rifle of the 17th and most of the 18th Century was usually some form of breech loader. It was not until after the American War ended in 1783 that muzzle loading rifles came into general favour with the small portion of the population who had any use for a rifle at all. This type of screw-plug mechanism is known as the La Chaumette system, after the Frenchman who patented the basic idea in 1700, and again when he came to England in 1721. The breechplug was completely removed and the powder poured in first, followed by the ball, after which the plug was re-introduced and turned home by several turns of the guard

Left: the double side-by-side gun did not become popular in English sporting circles until the Regency period, when it rapidly displaced the single gun. This graceful gun by Stephen Sandwell of London, circa 1765, shows the basic design of the English fowling piece just past the mid-century mark. The long round wrist and shape of the butt are as they had been for the previous fifty years, but the barrel is coming to be held by the flat key or slide, and the surface of the lockplate and cock are usually flat from the end of the 1750s. The Spanish-form or half-octagon barrel is typical. A gun built specially for a left-handed shooter is, however, very unusual

Far left: this silver-mounted sporting gun by Chasteau of Paris, bearing hallmarks for 1772 shows a high quality French gun in the style of the final years of the ancien régime before the Revolution brought the neo-classical style into a prominence which would last until the early percussion period

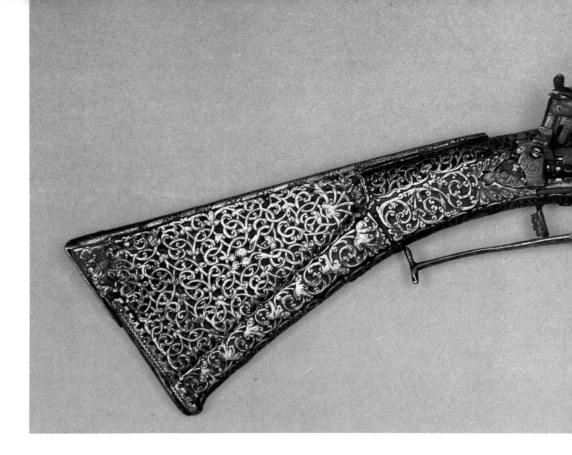

The shape of the butt, and trigger guard, and the use of the miquelet lock, combined with the pierced steel inlay which covers the stock identify this musket as Sardinian, dating about the middle of the 18th Century. The basic form of Sardinian arms did not change from the time of the wheel-lock, and this profusely decorated example is an excellent representative piece

An early 18th Century sporting gun of obscure origins. The silver encrusted barrel and lock are decorated with flowers and subjects from Indian mythology; the style of the butt is early, but if the weapon is Indian in origin it might have been stocked in an outmoded fashion in the middle of the century

breech-loading and rifled arms, very often combined in one weapon. The origins of both these features so far as they apply to English 17th Century arms are obscure, and not particularly associated with the larger overall Dutch influence prevalent at the time of their introduction. Rifling was at this time employed almost exclusively by southern German and Austrian gun makers, while breech loading had no particular area of popularity, unless of course England itself be considered.

Breechloading arms had been made in England for Henry VIII, and had been used in the construction of cannon almost from the introduction of heavy ordnance. But the first widespread use of breech loading arms was certainly in England during the final thirty years of the 17th Century. These most often took the form of rifled pistols and carbines, and to a far smaller degree, fowling pieces. These were constructed on what is now termed the

A curiously styled gun of Dutch origin, about 1685. The snaphaunce lock has the cock in the form of a swan, with its jaws holding the flint, with another smaller swan gripping the steel. The damascus barrel, lock, and iron furniture are all silver encrusted and decorated with grotesque animals and foliage. The butt is fluted almost in the Madrid manner, but the overall effect is Germanic

30

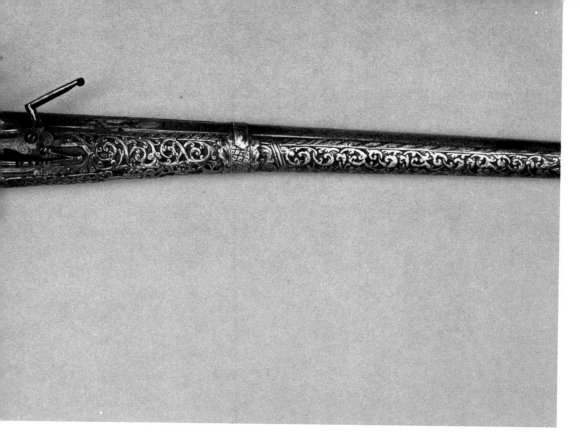

'turn-off' principle, wherein the breech section is heavily made and bored with a chamber which is filled with powder and the ball placed on top of it. The barrel, having previously been unscrewed from the breech, is then replaced and screwed up tight. It was a ideal system for combining with a rifled barrel, since the ball could be made slightly larger than bore diameter and thus obtain perfect obturation and grip upon the rifling without deforming of the ball during loading – neither of which could be satisfactorily achieved with a muzzle loading rifled arm.

By the second quarter of the 18th Century rifling was less commonly used on English pistols, dying out almost entirely by about 1750, but the 'turn-off' system continued in use for pocket pistols until the middle of the 19th Century. Until the last quarter of the 18th Century English rifles were almost entirely constructed on one of several breech-loading designs, but then reverted almost as completely to the muzzle loading principle. With very few exceptions, fowling pieces were made throughout the period from the Restoration until the acceptance of the pin- and central fire breech loader, as ordinary muzzle loading arms. These followed the Dutch and then the French pattern through the third quarter of the 18th Century, finally developing into the classic modern sporting gun design during the early years of the 19th Century. It was not until the 1820s, however, that the double-barrelled gun firmly supplanted the single sporting gun in England.

Although the basic construction of the flintlock remained virtually unchanged throughout its long life on all forms of personal and military arms, a very great number of stylistic renderings were made upon the several features, and a large number of refinements, improvements and minor alterations in design and operation were carried out by Western European gun makers. It is by means of these refinements and stylistic developments that we are able to identify otherwise unmarked or undated examples. Amongst the most important of these features may be included the following:

1. The tumbler bridle, which acted as a guide and a support for the movement of the tumbler and the sear. This appeared on French locks about 1660, and on English weapons during the first quarter of the 18th Century.
2. The pan bridle, consisting of an arm integral with the flash-pan extending forward and acting as an outer support for the steel pivot screw. This appeared generally during the first quarter of the 18th Century, but

The ill-fated Ferguson rifle, patented in 1776 and used for a few months during the American War, was an adaptation of a French system first patented in 1700. Both types enjoyed popularity as sporting rifles, more breech-loaders being produced in England than muzzle-loading rifles during the 18th Century. Rifles of the La Chaumette and the Ferguson systems continued to be made into the 1820s in small numbers, but the muzzle loading rifle predominated in England after the American War. The rifle shown here is of the style described as 'Officer's rifle' from its military form combined with higher quality furniture and decoration

31

An example of the neo-classical First Empire style in gunmaking, this presentation sporting gun was made in 1802 by Nicholas-Noel Boutet as part of a gift of arms from the Consulate to the King of Spain, Charles IV. Silver furniture, fire-blued barrel with gold inlay, gold relief decoration on the bright-finish lock, and extremely detailed relief carving of the stock make this a superb example of the Boutet style

particularly in Germany and Austria did not come into widespread use until the end of the century. Locks possessing both of these additional supports were more costly than ordinary locks, and were usually termed 'double-bridle locks'.

3. Sliding safety catch, normally fitted into the tail of the lockplate, operating in one or more ways to prevent the movement of the cock until released by drawing backwards. Some 'bolts' as they are usually called, acted only upon the inside surface of the cock, while others acted on the tumbler itself; still others had a forward extension which fitted into a small hole in the base of the steel and locked this member as well. This latter addition is particularly common on pistols. This device appeared in the late 17th Century, and enjoyed differing lengths of popularity in various countries. In England, for instance, it was much used during the third quarter of the 18th Century, but went quickly out of use on fowling pieces after that time, although continued on rifle and pistol locks into the percussion period.

4. The raised pan, with the surrounding fence pierced to allow water to run off more easily, appeared about 1740, but only on high quality arms. It never came into general use on military flintlocks although several countries partially adopted it early in the 19th Century. This is usually called the 'semi-waterproof pan' and was sometimes accompanied by the mating surface of the pan-cover being grooved and recessed to fit over the lip of the slightly raised pan.

5. Anti-friction rollers, fitted at first to the toe of the steel and later to the tip of the upper limb of the steel spring, made their appearance about the middle of the 18th Century, and were widely adopted for all forms of quality arms in England and France, but, like the pan bridle, did not make much impression in Germany and Austria, or Spain, until the close of the century. Locks fitted with one of these devices are usually described as locks with 'roller steels' or 'roller steel springs'.

6. Another anti-friction device, the detent, came into limited use at about the same period, particularly in association with arms having set or hair triggers. This was a small lever pivoted on the outer face of the tumbler which caught the tip of the sear as the tumbler was falling, and prevented the sear from catching in the half-cock notch. Locks so fitted could be adjusted for a very light trigger pull. This device saw fully as much use on German weapons as on those of other countries, even being fitted to some military arms in the 1780s.

7. The final anti-friction device to make its appearance on the flintlock was the swivel mainspring, which incorporated a small link between the tumbler and the tip of the mainspring, so that the bearing points were very greatly reduced. Although widely adopted on weapons of quality, the older hook mainspring remained in use on poorer quality arms and on most military arms. Swivel mainsprings appeared just after the turn of the mid-century.

Other improvements associated with flintlock arms but not involved in the lock itself include the use of gold to line, at first, vent or touchhole, and later, pans as well. In both cases it was intended to prevent erosion of the iron by the hot gas and chemical action of the burning powder. From 1805 the use of platinum replaced gold for these purposes on English arms, especially on ligh quality arms. Gold-lined vents appeared as early as around 1725 on Spanish barrels.

Two other features affecting the barrel were the break-off, false, or hook-breech, and the substitution of slides for pins in securing the barrel to the stock. This latter feature came into general use as the result of the introduction of the break-off breech. The break-off breech consisted of a separate breech, or standing breech, which screwed into the stock like an ordinary tang, but had a section ahead of the tang parallel with the breech of the barrel. The

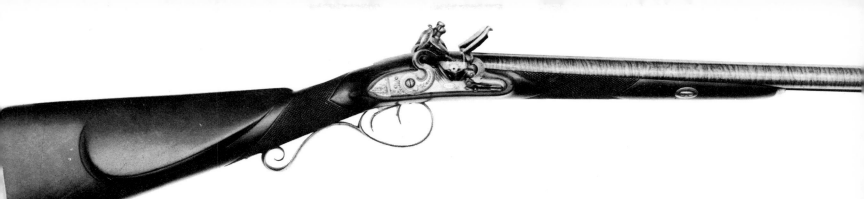

breechplug was made with a hook or hut, rather than a tang strap as formerly, and this hook fitted into a cavity in the face of the standing breech. This feature, when used in conjunction with keys, allowed far easier removal of the barrel for cleaning or carriage without any attendant risk of damage to the stock.

Despite these various refinements and improvements, the flintlock as an ignition system still possessed serious faults which could not, in the nature of things, be completely remedied. The flint was the source of ignition, and even best quality flints were liable to break or chip at the crucial moment; in any event they had to be changed every twenty to fifty shots – depending upon how cautious the shooter was, and how good his flints. The vent or passage between the flash-pan and the main charge was liable to clogging from powder fouling, and had to be attended to. Regardless of the precision introduced into the mechanism there was still a time-lag on the vast majority of locks. Priming powder, if left in the pan for any length of time, became damp and unreliable, and required frequent changing. And of course the pan flash of smoke tended to obscure sight of the target, whether man, bird, or beast.

All of these impediments were, quite naturally, accepted at the time by the vast majority of those whose employment or pleasure depended upon fire-arms, and it was only through the efforts of a very small group of academic experimenters that a new system was discovered which ultimately remedied the several faults inherent in the flintlock. And even this new system took a quarter of a century to achieve general acceptance and to reach a state where it was a genuine step forward. The flintlock died the hardest of any of the several ignition systems on firearms, but this is perhaps not so surprising when it is recalled that it lasted longer than any of the others – from about 1630 to about 1830.

A fine example of the English double gun of the early 19th Century, a period usually considered as being the finest in the English gun making trade. The fine balance and handling qualities, the superb finish of all the components, and the mechanical excellence of the mechanisms gave a weapon its individual claim to excellence in sharp contrast to the contemporary European standards which concentrated much more on the excellence of the design and execution of the decoration. This example by Bass was made at the turn of the century

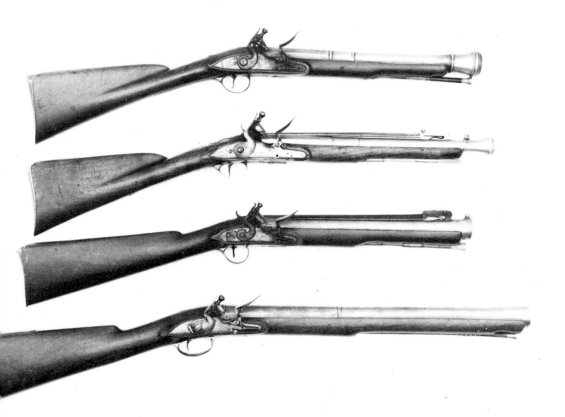

The high degree of development in public transport – with an increase in coaching inns – and the great expansion of British sea power in the 18th Century both created situations in which the blunderbuss proved an ideal weapon. The four examples shown here span the 18th Century, and two of them carry spring-bayonets which could be used by tavern keepers in close combat with drunken mobs. Brass barrels and furniture were normally used for naval blunderbusses, but coaching guns are also found with these decorative (and cheaper) features

The blunderbuss. Before leaving the flintlock we must notice one weapon intimately and peculiarly associated with this form of ignition: the blunderbuss. Although introduced to history in the middle of the 16th Century in Germany, as wheel-locks, and used in varying degrees throughout Europe, this arm is strongly connected with 18th Century England.

There are many legendsand misconceptions connected with the blunderbuss and its use, but it is no exaggeration to say that the actual history of this arm is probably even more 'romantic' than the legends. At first designed for use by mounted troops, it achieved its greatest popularity as a naval and coaching weapon. The flared muzzle, although it did not give the shot any wider spread, did provide a much easier means of loading from a moving surface, such as the deck or rigging of a ship at sea, or a coach lurching along bad roads. The psychological effect must have come into it as well, for there is ample evidence of its use by householders and tavern-keepers as a property defense weapon. The blunderbuss was normally manufactured in carbine length, and frequently with a brass barrel as well as the conventional iron.

From the third quarter of the 18th Century English blunderbusses were often made with some form of spring-activated bayonet, and pistols were also made with flared muzzles and spring-bayonets. Larger blunderbusses were made for use in ship's boats, and these were generally fitted with a row-lock through the forearm, and were mounted in the bow of such boats, for use in covering an amphibious assault or attacking another boat or ship.

Blunderbusses were loaded with pistol balls or smaller sized shot. Military versions were loaded with specific numbers of ball depending upon the bore size. They were never normally loaded with the legendary handful of stones, broken glass and bits of metal, as this would have quickly ruined the barrel, and doubtless jammed and caused the barrel to blow up.

Blunderbusses continued to be made, particularly for the oriental market, until about the middle of the 19th Century, but with the coming of the railways to Britain, and the close of large-scale naval warfare in 1815, the weapon lost most of the reasons for existence in western Europe. In some instances the cheap double-barrelled sporting gun which came into prominence as the result of the ease of manufacture of the percussion system, probably replaced the blunderbuss in several of its protective functions. The blunderbuss died a social death, passing away with the scene in which it had thrived.

Development of the rifle. The 18th Century witnessed the development of firearms in a new area of the world, one which was ultimately to make

A Spanish miquelet-lock sporting gun, but with a Madrid style stock. This gun is by Matthias Quero of Malaga, and the barrel is dated 1742. Note the larger lockplate, and the more elaborate furniture of this arm compared to the previous gun. The French style of butt was never popular in Spain, either the Madrid or Catalan styles being used to the virtual exclusion of all others

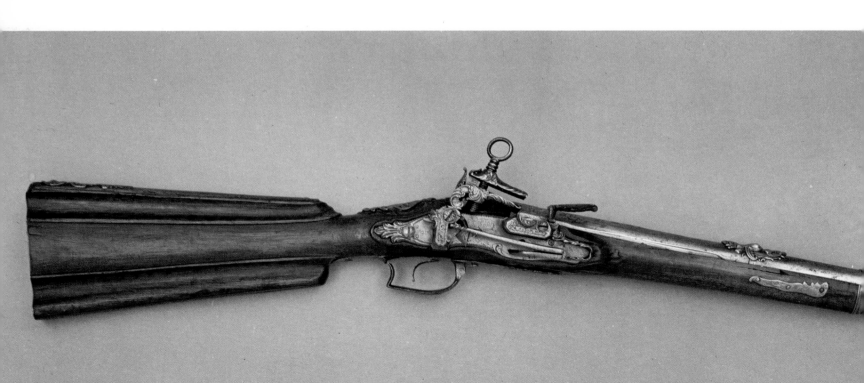

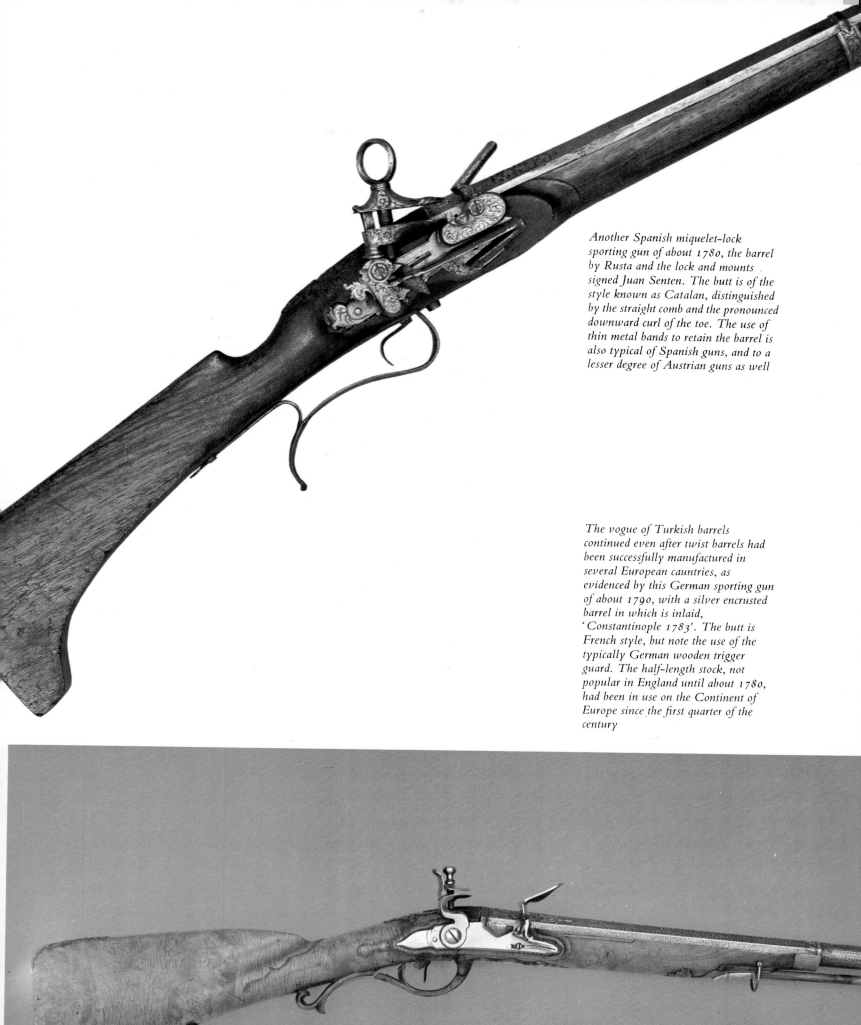

Another Spanish miquelet-lock sporting gun of about 1780, the barrel by Rusta and the lock and mounts signed Juan Senten. The butt is of the style known as Catalan, distinguished by the straight comb and the pronounced downward curl of the toe. The use of thin metal bands to retain the barrel is also typical of Spanish guns, and to a lesser degree of Austrian guns as well

The vogue of Turkish barrels continued even after twist barrels had been successfully manufactured in several European cauntries, as evidenced by this German sporting gun of about 1790, with a silver encrusted barrel in which is inlaid, 'Constantinople 1783'. The butt is French style, but note the use of the typically German wooden trigger guard. The half-length stock, not popular in England until about 1780, had been in use on the Continent of Europe since the first quarter of the century

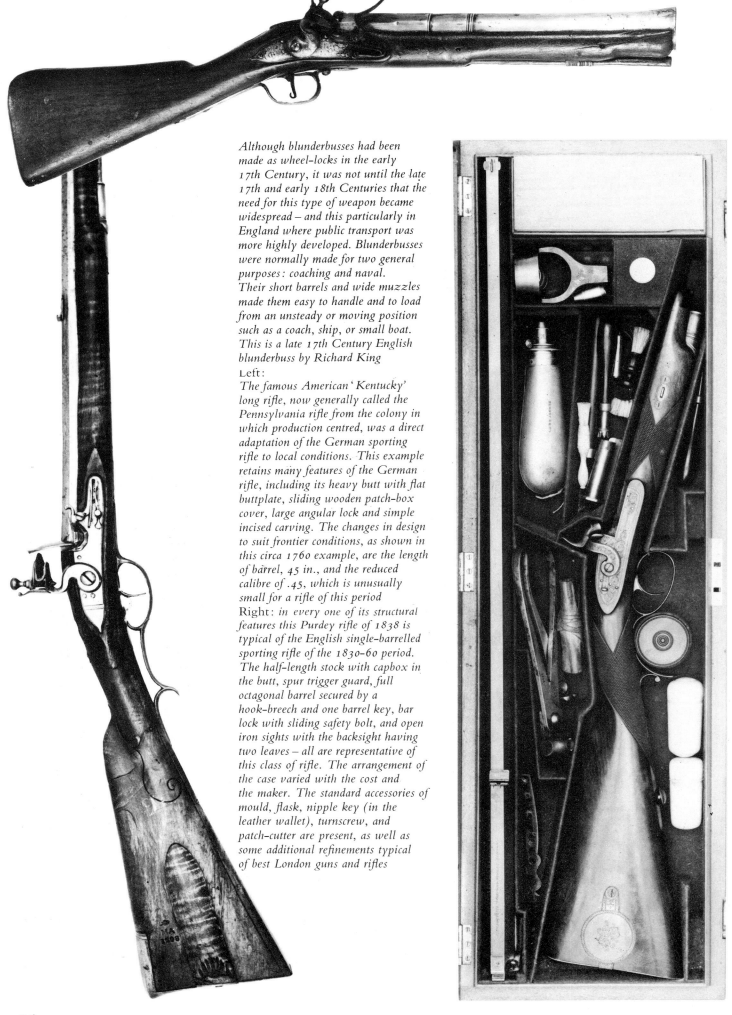

Although blunderbusses had been made as wheel-locks in the early 17th Century, it was not until the late 17th and early 18th Centuries that the need for this type of weapon became widespread – and this particularly in England where public transport was more highly developed. Blunderbusses were normally made for two general purposes: coaching and naval. Their short barrels and wide muzzles made them easy to handle and to load from an unsteady or moving position such as a coach, ship, or small boat. This is a late 17th Century English blunderbuss by Richard King

Left:
The famous American 'Kentucky' long rifle, now generally called the Pennsylvania rifle from the colony in which production centred, was a direct adaptation of the German sporting rifle to local conditions. This example retains many features of the German rifle, including its heavy butt with flat buttplate, sliding wooden patch-box cover, large angular lock and simple incised carving. The changes in design to suit frontier conditions, as shown in this circa 1760 example, are the length of barrel, 45 in., and the reduced calibre of .45, which is unusually small for a rifle of this period

Right: in every one of its structural features this Purdey rifle of 1838 is typical of the English single-barrelled sporting rifle of the 1830-60 period. The half-length stock with capbox in the butt, spur trigger guard, full octagonal barrel secured by a hook-breech and one barrel key, bar lock with sliding safety bolt, and open iron sights with the backsight having two leaves – all are representative of this class of rifle. The arrangement of the case varied with the cost and the maker. The standard accessories of mould, flask, nipple key (in the leather wallet), turnscrew, and patch-cutter are present, as well as some additional refinements typical of best London guns and rifles

tremendous contributions to the manufacture and proliferation of firearms – America. From the time of the first settlements on the Atlantic seaboard in 1607, such firearms as were possessed by the colonists were imported from England as personal possessions or colonial property. With the increased immigration of Germans which began about the turn of the century, a new element was introduced. Most of these colonists landed at the port of Philadelphia and settled in the colony of Pennsylvania. Some brought with them their sporting rifles, generally known as 'jaeger rifles', and it appears that some of these men were gun makers by trade.

Local conditions and requirements saw the rapid evolution of a peculiarly American arm descended directly from the German jaeger rifle. This has variously been called the 'Kentucky' rifle and the 'Pennsylvania' rifle, but during the 18th Century it was generally referred to as the American long rifle, which describes it quite accurately without entering into the limitations of regional definitions. The salient features of this environmentally developed weapon included a long heavy barrel, normally fully octagonal but sometimes of 'Spanish form' or half-octagonal, with a rifled bore of from .66 to .50 on the average for the period prior to the American War for Independence. Subsequently the calibre was reduced to about .45 to .40 and even smaller during the first half of the 19th Century, by which time it had lost its individual identity.

The American long rifle was decorated with brass furniture in contrast to the bone, wood, and brass used on the German prototypes, although the earliest examples had sliding wood butt-trap covers as did the German rifles. But the subsequent use of brass for the trap-cover after about 1760 is one of the uniquely American contributions to the arm, along with its long and heavy barrel. During the last half of the century they came to be decorated with rococo scroll carving, and were generally fitted with double set triggers.

Despite the tremendous prominence into which this arm was brought as the result of the American War, it is nevertheless true that it formed a very small part of the total number of firearms in America during the 18th Century, the greater part of which was comprised of muskets and fowling pieces almost entirely imported from England. Local gunsmithing concentrated upon the production of rifles in the frontier areas, and in stocking and repairing weapons which had originated in Europe. The high cost of labour kept the production of firearms in America to a minimum until the design and introduction of machinery capable of producing interchangeable parts allowed for expansion. It was not until the American Civil War of 1861–5 that private industry began to manufacture firearms on a truly large scale.

Throughout the 18th Century there were few innovations in the design of the rifle, except in America as described above. Its use on a limited scale was adopted by the armies of most European countries except France by the time of the Seven Years' War. Frederick II of Prussia established the first permanent rifle corps in 1740, and rifles generally in use during the century were closely patterned on the German model: short, large-calibre octagonal barrel with a thick heavy full-length stock. While the long rifle of the Americans had a tremendous psychological effect upon their British and German foes, this effect was not long-lived, and had little effect upon the overall design of the military rifle of the 18th Century, or upon the organisation of armies with respect to the rifle. As a muzzle-loading military arm, the rifle did not become practical for large-scale use until the development of the expanding cylindro-conoidal bullet by Delvigne and Minié in the 1840s.

The percussion system. Experiments with fulminating powder had been carried on during the 18th Century, primarily in France, but all ultimately culminated in the experimenters blowing up guns or themselves. The Scottish Reverend Alexander Forsyth was the first experimenter to apply his efforts to a priming charge rather than to a propellant charge. He discovered

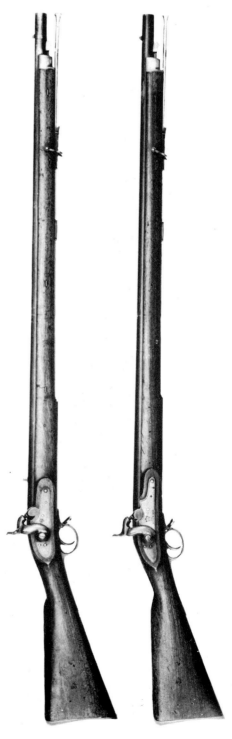

From the beginning of the 1830s the percussion ignition system was gradually adopted by the governments of the world for their military small arms, but flintlocks remained in use in some armies, usually militia or reserves, into the 1850s. England's first percussion musket for the line infantry was the Pattern 1839 (below left), which differed little in design from the earlier flintlock arms. The first new-production percussion musket intended for the infantry was the Pattern 1842 (below right), and both types saw extensive service in the Crimean War

that chlorate of potash would ignite powder charges if itself ignited by a blow rather than a spark, and by 1805 he had developed a lock which would accomplish this task. During 1806 and 1807 Forsyth carried on further experiments at the expense of the British Government in the Tower of London, and having concluded this work, he was granted a patent in April, 1807.

The basic difficulty with Forsyth's system was that, while it was more sure-fire than the flintlock, it differed little in the complication of the mechanism, was more troublesome to clean and operate efficiently, and tended to get out of order rather easily. So that, while in principle it represented a great step forward, in practice it was almost as impractical as the flintlock. There is no question that if alternative applications of the percussion principle had not been made, the system probably would have faded into oblivion. These alternatives took the form of the tube-lock, and the copper cap, although there were a number of others.

Joseph Manton was first on the scene with the tube-lock in 1818, but the precise credit for the copper cap will probably never be known; there were too many claimants at the same time. It seems probable however that Josha Shaw's use of the iron, pewter, and finally copper cap was seized upon by Joseph Egg and first commercialized by that gun maker. But the key factor was the substitution of fulminate of mercury for chlorate of potash, which occurred as the result of work and publicity by E. Goode Wright of Hereford, in 1823. When this was applied to the copper cap, or to tubes, it gave a reliable, waterproof, relatively non-corrosive primer. It is to Mr Wright that posterity probably owes the greatest debt of gratitude for making the percussion principle of Forsyth a chemically practical system.

The adoption of the percussion ignition system in one form or another by the non-military shooting element by about 1830 produced little change in the overall appearance of firearms. Most of the styles had been settled during the long reign of the flintlock, and it was not until the mechanism of the breech-loader tended to separate the fore-end from the buttstock (what the English called the 'American system' of stocking) that great changes in the appearance of small arms occurred.

The production of highly decorated firearms declined steadily from the beginning of the 19th Century, not only because there were fewer people to give or to receive such arms, but because firearms came increasingly to be regarded as mechanical devices rather than as elements for artistic expression. Mechanical ingenuity and exquisite finish, delicate and finely executed engraving, functional excellence, and refined elegance tended to supplant the earlier lavish carving, inlay of silver and gold, gilding, and relief engraving.

It was not until the decade of the 1830s that the military authorities of Europe and America began to give serious consideration to the question of replacing the flintlock with the percussion gun. In most instances there was the dual problem of the economic aspect and settling upon a mechanism suitably substantial to withstand the rigours of military service. The individual sportsman could afford to tinker with an expensive and delicate mechanism: governments could afford neither. So it was not until the 1840s that the percussion lock began to be placed in the hands of the troops. While various precise dates for the adoption of the percussion lock could be given for the different countries, these would have little bearing upon the dates when such arms were in the hands of the troops, which is, after all, the essential point. Two instances will illustrate this point. While England partially adopted the percussion system in 1836, and wholly in 1838, the flintlock was still in the hands of some regiments in 1848. Again, the United States partially adopted the system in 1833, and wholly in 1841, but the Mexican War of 1846-8 was fought primarily with flintlock arms.

In doing away with the several pieces of external mechanism of the flintlock, and making the application of priming a far simpler and more compact process, the percussion system opened the way for the commercial

A sporting gun by Bongard of Düsseldorf, circa 1700, in which a Turkish silver-inlaid damascus barrel has been used. These barrels were captured in large numbers after the defeat of the Turks before Vienna in 1683, and are traditionally accepted as having introduced the twist barrel to Europe. Genuine Turkish damascus barrels were used on the finest quality Austrian weapons through the first quarter of the 18th Century, and some, as this western German example indicates, found their way to other countries, including England. Note the very plain stock, and the wooden trigger guard

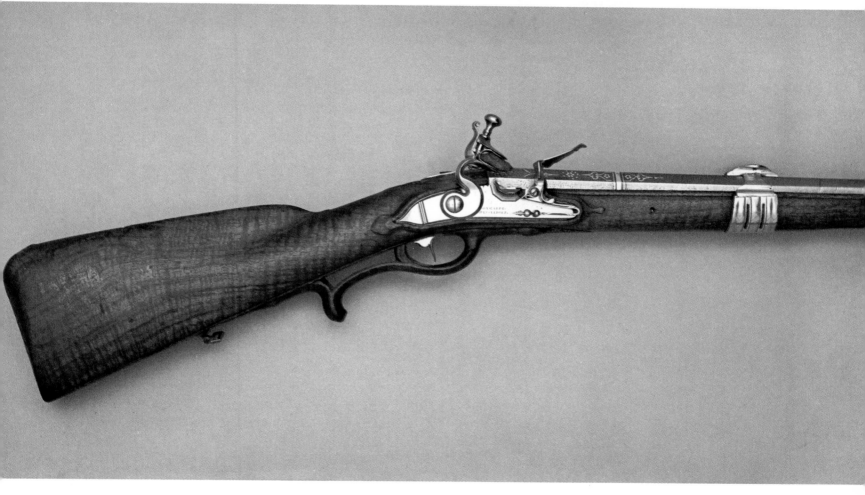

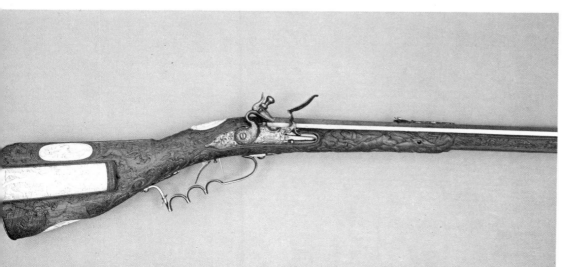

An early combination of the French lock and French butt with Germanic furniture and decoration is shown on this rifle made by Franz Ruef of Elwangen in 1697. Since Elwangen is located in Württemberg, and southern Germany was strongly influenced by French designs, this combination is understandable. The inlay work is ivory, and the surfaces of ivory, wood and metal – excepting the barrel – are profusely and elaborately carved and chiselled

Although the French led the way in the development of rifled military arms during the first half of the 19th Century, their own issue service arms remained wedded to the tactical realities of the past. With the exception of the innovation of the back-action lock which appeared on their first percussion infantry musket (Model 1842) and all subsequent percussion regulation arms, most of the furniture and overall design dated back to the Model 1777. Rifling was not adopted for the line infantry musket until the Model 1857, and no French percussion rifle-musket was fitted with an elevating backsight; this advance waiting until the introduction of the breechloader. This Model 1854 Rifle Musket for the Imperial Guards is improved over current infantry muskets only in having the rifled bore

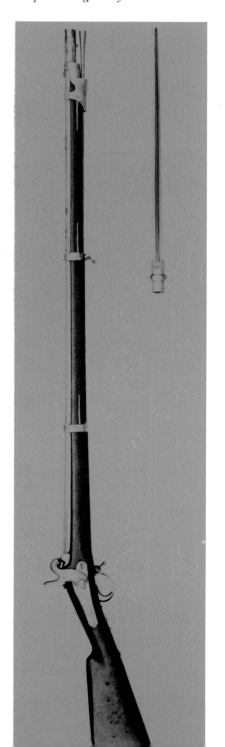

development of several ideas which had been thought of centuries earlier but held in abeyance by the complication of the flintlock ignition system. Primary amongst these pregnant ideas were the breech loader and the revolving chamber. Both dated back virtually to the original development of small arms, and both had seen considerable development in connexion with earlier firing mechanisms. But it required, apart from the compactness of the percussion system, the vastly increased powers of publicity, mechanical perfection and industrial organization which formed part of the industrial and social revolutions of the first half of the 19th Century, for these systems to achieve popular acknowledgement and commercial viability. It is not surprising therefore that both were first successfully exploited in the machine-oriented industrial complex of the United States, where the whole approach to the manufacture of anything was geared to mass production by factory units containing within their make-up the administrative and public relations organisation to make such production a paying proposition.

It is true enough that Samuel Colt's initial introduction of the revolving pistol failed after six years, and was only rescued by the advent of a war and the the importunities of individuals for the renewed production of such arms, on a much improved design; but the point is that the factory unit and organisation were available – in Eli Whitney's plant in Connecticut – to undertake this production on a paying basis, and Colt did not let this second chance slip by. His subsequent success was largely due to salesmanship, forceful personality, administrative and industrial organisation and the use of machinery in the basic stages of production which kept the cost down and the quantities up. The overall significance of the Colt revolver has been very greatly exaggerated by nationalistic fervour and romantic drama, but its impact upon the mid-Victorian industrial scene represents one of the real milestones in the development and synthesis of public relations, selling techniques, administrative and mechanical organisation.

The success of the breech loading arm was much the same. The Lorenzoni, screw-plug or La Chaumette, and Ferguson systems all suffered an early demise due to lack of publicity and mechanical crudities which did not allow their proliferation had there been a market for them. John Hall's breechloader of 1811, adopted by the American Government in 1819 and produced until 1844 as a flintlock rifle for the US Army, was the first successful breechloader and was manufactured on the interchangeable principle in a government armoury as well as by several private factories. Despite this it was not popular due to mechanical failings and was not commercially produced. The first commercially successful breech loading arm was that of Christian Sharps, patented in 1848 and produced in quantity from 1852. This again was an interchangeable weapon, and owed its existence to the facilities of Robbins & Lawrence, one of the two American firms who ultimately supplied the interchangeable machinery for the Enfield factory in 1856.

There were a vast number of British and Continental breech loading mechanisms and revolving chamber weapons manufactured, but no one system obtained a serious commercial grip upon the market because it was not produced in interchangeable quantities and adequately publicized. The Adams and Tranter revolving pistols in England, and the Lefaucheaux pin-fire revolving pistol on the Continent came as close to the American level of production as any, but here again it is doubtful whether any one firm reaped the commercial benefits which must have accrued to the establishment which could combine mass production to meet the demand with a public relations approach to create that demand. Westley Richards' 'monkey tail' percussion breech loader probably came closest to the mark in England and during the last half of the 19th Century a number of firms on the Continent were organised upon such principles as ensured large-scale success, but this development did not take place during the muzzle loading period of firearms evolution.

Cased pair of transition revolving pistols by John Blissett of London, circa 1852. Mechanically these were often merely pepperbox pistols to which a fixed barrel was joined, and the majority were not of good quality. The mechanical unreliability and delicacy of many of these transition revolvers may account for the early popularity of the far more robust and simple Colt series. This pair of revolvers by Blissett is of far higher quality than the average of its type and represents a type of handgun which gave the Colt serious competition outside of America until the 1860s

The progress made in industrial organization through the introduction of machinery and exploitation via the written word should be kept in prospective. For the major portion of the 19th Century the largest centres for the production of all types of firearms for world markets were Liege and Birmingham, where machinery was to some extent employed, but always secondarily to hand labour. The successful use of machinery pre-supposed the constant demand for large numbers of firearms of one pattern, i.e. military orders on governmental scale, and most of the American firms which had made such promising starts in mass production gun-making came to grief before the end of the century for lack of such large contracts. Arms-making centres which relied on hand labour could eke out existence on a constant flow of orders on a very much smaller scale because of the far lower overhead costs and cheapness of labour.

Readers may have noted the use of the term 'revolving pistol' in the above discussion: this was the contemparary term for what is now called the 'revolver' while this latter term referred to what we now call the 'pepperbox'. The pepperbox was the pre-industrial manifestation of the revolving chamber arm, and it enjoyed far more popularity than is generally realized. In fact, there is no question that there were far more pepperboxes sold than Colt's or other percussion revolving pistols during the muzzle loading period, and that they enjoyed world-wide sales. The years 1852-4 were known as 'the Australian years' in the Birmingham gun trade from the vast numbers of pepperboxes exported to that continent alone.

Another confusing term describing a much misunderstood weapon is 'transition revolver.' In *design* these pistols are a transitional development between the pepperbox and the revolving pistol, being mechanically more of a pepperbox with the revolving barrel unit shortened to a cylinder with a barrel added at the front. But chronologically the transition revolver was produced concurrently with the pepperbox from the early 1850s, and with the several patterns of American and English revolving pistols until about 1860.

A cased 'pepperbox' revolver by Joseph Lang, circa 1845. This was the first 'revolver' and the term was used to distinguish it from the 'revolving pistol' which term described the Colt and other revolving-chamber arms with fixed barrels. From the early 1840s this type of pistol became very popular with immigrants and in the colonies as a personal defence weapon. Unlike the majority of the pepperboxes, this example is of very high quality. They were manufactured in large quantities in Birmingham, Liege, and to a lesser extent in America

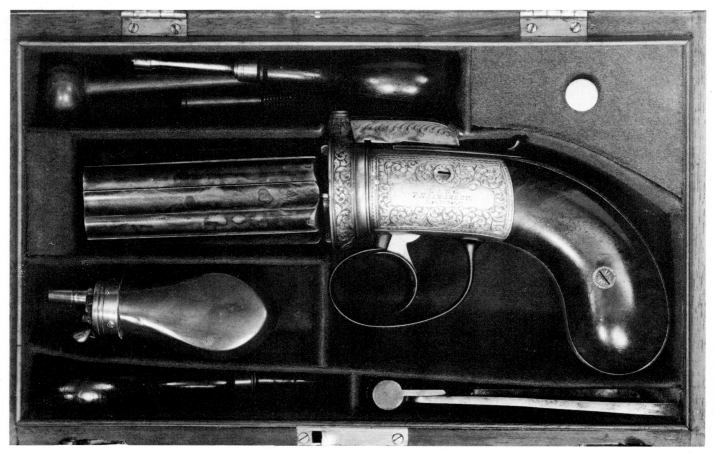

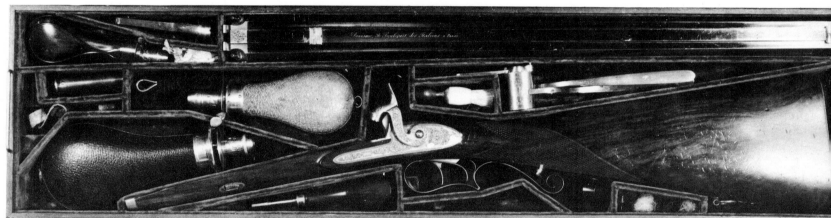

The industrial organisation and expansion of the first half of the 19th Century, along with great improvements in communication and transportation, made the spread and interchange of ideas possible on a scale never previously achieved. Technological advances made the waging of war a more complex operation, and the failure of tactics and strategy to keep pace with technology created the holocausts of the Crimean and American Civil Wars. The impetus to invention stimulated by these conflicts resulted in the commercial development of the self-contained metallic cartridge which in turn made the repeating rifle a sensible production, and this deadly trio was completed with the development of smokeless powder which made its appearance on the military scene in the mid-1880s. The day of the artistic firearm, of superb hand craftsmanship and elegant design was setting; the day of the ever more deadly mechanical implement was dawning.

For at least two decades after the introduction of the percussion system in France, the design of sporting arms continued to follow the First Empire style epitomised by Boutet and Lepage, but by the 1840s a more restrained style was coming into favour. By 1850, the date of this cased pair of gun and rifle by Devisme, it was not unusual for the leading French makers to style their arms on English models in which the emphasis was upon grace of line and elegance of finish instead of lavishness of ornamentation.
The French called the pattern of lock used here the 'isolated' lock, known in England as the Westley Richards' lock, and apparently introduced in that country by Charles Moore in 1827

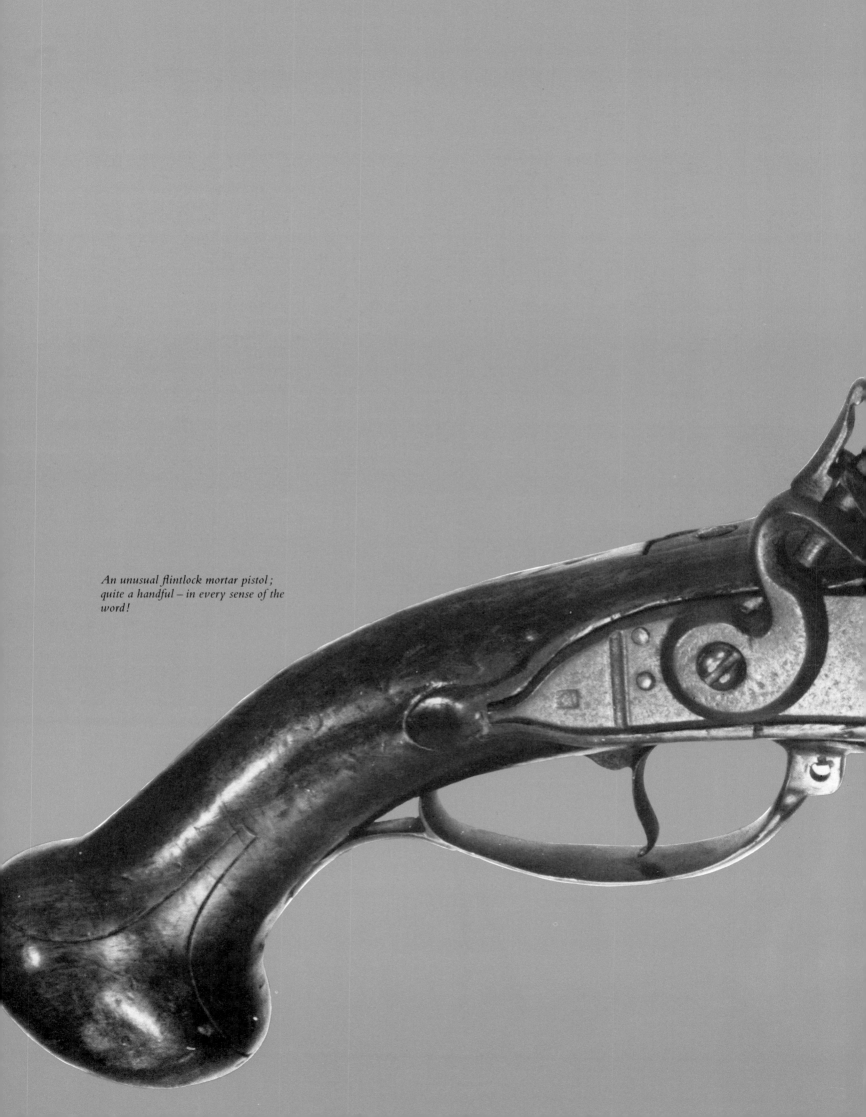

*An unusual flintlock mortar pistol;
quite a handful – in every sense of the
word!*

CHAPTER III

CURIOSA

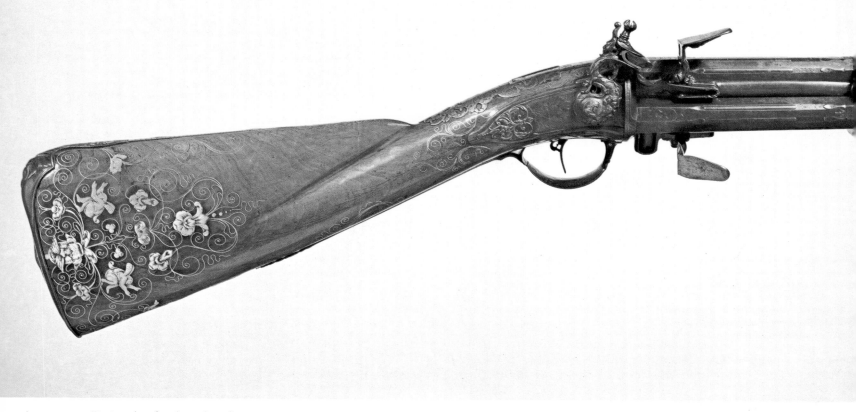

Designed to fire three shots from one loading this beautiful French gun is decorated with silver inlay whilst the mounts are finely chiselled. Barrel 31.3 inches, bore .59 inches, weight 7 lb. 6 oz.

Detail of previous item – each chamber was loaded with shot and powder and the attached pan was primed. One chamber was in line with the barrel after this shot had been discharged, the cylinder block was rotated to bring the second chamber into the firing position. The lock had to be re-cocked before each charge could be fired

Although the introduction of gunpowder must have seemed a tremendous innovation to 14th Century militarists, it was not without its limitations. Apart from the physical difficulties involved in the mixing, transportation, and storing of gunpowder, the weapons themselves were limited. Firearms needed to be loaded before each shot and even then efficient action could not be guaranteed. Once he had fired, the gunner was at risk and liable to attack by quick moving cavalry before he could reload. This problem was to bedevil the designers of firearms right up to the middle of the 19th Century when repeating firearms first became really practical. Until that date many efforts, ingenious and often impractical, were made with varying degrees of success.

Multi-shot weapons. One obvious solution was to fit the gun with several barrels and from the very beginning handguns were produced with three or four barrels, each fired independently. This use of multiple barrels became common practice and pistols and longarms with two or more barrels were produced throughout the centuries using every form of detonation.

From the 16th Century onwards the most popular system was to mount two barrels, one above the other; the barrel block was locked into position by some form of catch and after the top barrel had been fired the catch was released and the block rotated to bring up the unfired barrel. Gunsmiths made another approach to the problem by using one barrel and incorporating a series of chambers, making the weapon, in effect, a revolver. The problem with all such weapons was the difficulty of preventing a serious loss of power as the result of gas leakage at the point where chamber and barrel met. This difficulty was not really overcome until the introduction of cartridges and a greatly improved technology enabled the production of better fitting parts. In the case of flintlock weapons the necessity for a priming pan complicated the issue still further. Some designers sought to produce a system which would need only one frizzen to serve all barrels but it usually proved simpler to fit each barrel with its own pan and frizzen and then use a single cock.

With the introduction of the percussion cap and subsequently the cartridge, design problems were greatly reduced and the floodgates of invention were opened. One optimist, Joseph Enouy, designed a pepperbox revolver with a bar fitted between butt and barrel on to which was fitted a 'wheel' with seven cylinders, each cylinder holding six charges. As a cylinder was emptied so the wheel was rotated to bring a fresh one into line with the barrel and hammer. In theory the idea was sound but one shudders at the thought of the difficulties of carrying such a weapon let alone firing it.

Similar practical troubles must have dogged the unfortunate user of a weapon made by the London gunmaker, Henry Nock. This had a cylinder comprising seven barrels, all of which were discharged simultaneously. The thought of coping with such a weapon on the fighting tops of a pitching man-of-war, for that is where they were intended to be used, would surely have deterred any but the bravest.

Another approach to the problem of producing multishot firearms was that of using superimposed charges. The basic idea was simple; into the barrel went a charge of powder and ball and next came a thickish wad, followed by a second charge of powder and ball. The second charge was fired first and the wad prevented ignition of the other charge which could then be fired as and when required. However the design began to get involved when the ignition system was considered. It was most important that each charge was fired in sequence, consequently each required a separate touch-hole or nipple which had to be spaced along the barrel to correspond with each charge. The difficulty was thus to produce a lock mechanism with cock or hammer which was capable of reaching the spaced charges. Some makers avoided the problem by fitting separate locks adjacent to each charge

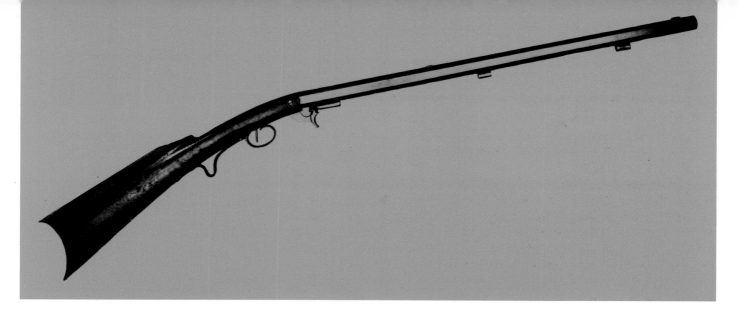

but this tended to make the weapon a little impractical although the alternative system of using a lock which was physically moved along the stock was not much better. Many and ingenious were the attempts to find a solution but few ever gained wide acceptance.

Combination weapons. If for any reason, perhaps cost or convenience, a multishot weapon was not acceptable, then it behoved a prudent man to provide himself with a second firearm or, alternatively, another weapon. Many gunmakers felt that an even better idea was to combine a firearm with another weapon of attack or defence. The bodyguard of Henry VIII (1509-1547) was at one time equipped with a small, round, steel shield at the centre of which was fitted an unusual breechloading matchlock pistol. A more fearsome combination was achieved by fitting several barrels into the head of a spiked club known, ironically, as a 'holy-water sprinkler'. More elegant perhaps, but hardly less brutal, were the slender maces fitted with a wheel-lock pistol – which of the weapons one was recommended to try first is uncertain. A rather unlikely combination was that of crossbow and wheel-lock which certainly seems to suggest a lack of confidence since both were missile weapons!

There can be no doubt that the most common type of combination weapon was the pistol sword, or sword pistol – the difference being which part of the weapon was considered to be of primary importance. The majority of such weapons appear to be of the hunting variety and were probably intended for administering the *coup-de-grâce* to a wounded animal. Most have a small barrel and simple lock mounted at the top of the blade just below the guard and the trigger is to be found inside the knuckle bow. A few specimens are found with two pistols fitted, one on either side of the blade and, far rarer are those with four barrels.

Basically similar to the sword pistols are the knife pistols which come in all sizes. Most have the barrel pointing along the blade but a few have the mechanism and barrel fitted into the hilt with the barrel pointing back directly at the user – a potentially dangerous arrangement. Although the great majority of knife pistols were civilian, some were acquired by the US Navy. In 1837 George Elgin patented a design for a 'Pistol-Knife' in which he sought to combine a bowie knife and a pistol. The result was a rather ugly looking weapon with a single-shot percussion pistol fitted with a broad knife blade beneath the barrel. These Elgin pistols vary in details such as the shape of the blade and the fitting of a bar across the butt on some to serve as a knuckle bow. One hundred and fifty of them were purchased by the Navy Department and were intended for use by a South Seas Exploring Expedition and cost, complete with a leather holster, seventeen dollars fifty cents each.

Far more convenient for the ordinary man who felt the need to carry a double-purpose weapon were the Unwin and Rodgers knife pistols. These

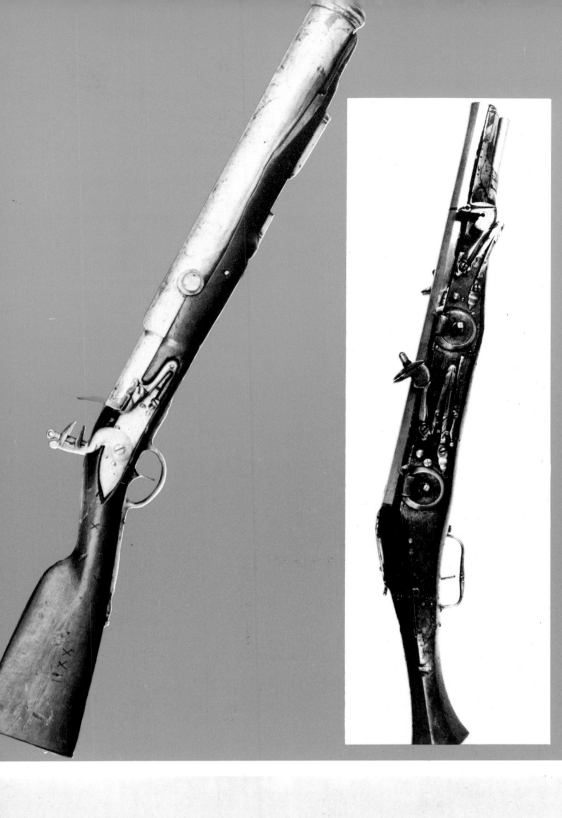

Attemps to overcome the limitations of early pistols and turn them into repeating weapons were numerous and this wheel-lock made around the middle of the 16th century, illustrates one of the commonest methods. It is fitted with three separate locks each of which fired one shot. The three charges were separated from each other by wads and were fired in reverse order of loading – the last to be loaded being the first to be discharged. Each lock was activated in turn by pressure on the trigger. Barrel 15.6 inches, bore .495 inches

Far left: Rather like a large blunderbuss in appearance, this swivel gun has two trunions to fit on to a support. It was designed to fire a type of shot known as 'langridge'. The barrel is engraved with the badge of the Admiralty of Amsterdam and is dated 1799. The fittings are all of brass. Barrel 21 inches, bore 1.2 inches

These unusual devices were used for firing signal flares. Powder was placed in the flat pans at the end of the stock and this was ignited by the flash produced by the percussion cap or the flintlock mechanism operated by the trigger

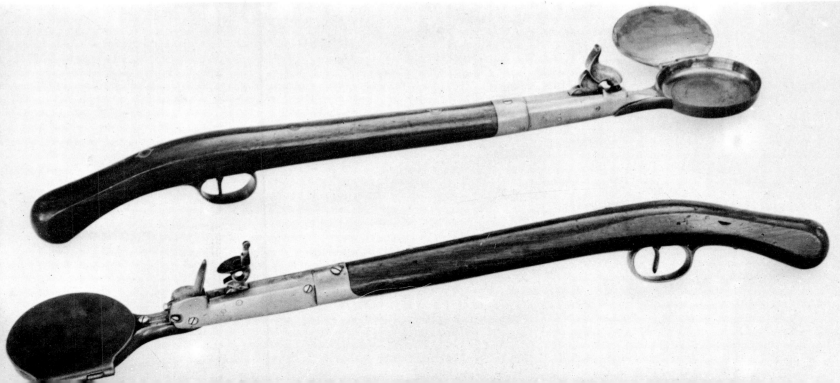

were essentially large pocket knives, usually with two blades, fitted along the back with a short barrel. The pistol was originally a percussion type using a cap but later models were loaded with a small cartridge. Some of the earlier models were adapted to house a minute bullet mould and a small ramrod and a few were produced which had two barrels.

If a larger pistol was preferred then a spring bayonet could be fitted to the barrel, an idea which was patented by John Waters in 1781. A bayonet of triangular section was pivotted at the muzzle of the weapon and when it was folded back a simple spring was compressed whilst the point of the blade was engaged with some form of catch. When the catch was released the tension of the spring forced the bayonet forward to swing over and lock into the extended position. Pressure on a side stud released the bayonet to be folded back when no longer required. Spring bayonets were fitted to pistols and blunderbusses, either above or below the barrel, although some will be found fitted on the side. As to their practical value there is little evidence for contemporary accounts seldom, if ever, mention them; possibly the determined swish and snap of a spring loaded blade snapping into position was sufficient deterrent to drive off any attacker.

The idea of a pivotting bayonet-like attachment was not forgotten and as late as the end of the 19th Century the so-called Apache pistol was fitted with one. This pocket-sized weapon was ingenious and vicious for it con-

Top: 'My Friend' was an all metal pistol designed to be held with the little finger passing through the hole in the butt and the body of the weapon gripped in the hand. Held thus it formed an unpleasant knuckleduster. Held as a revolver it could fire five shots and some models were fitted with a short barrel. The design was patented in 1865 by James Reid of New York
Bottom: this four-shot weapon, known as the Shatuck Unique, was patented in 1906 by O. Mossberg of Massachusetts. Four barrels were drilled in a single block which was released for loading by pressure on the catch at the top. Upward pressure on the butt fired each barrel in turn

50

Top: *known as an Apache knuckleduster pistol because of a supposed preference for it by Paris criminals, this was the multiple weapon par excellence. The grip, here shown unlatched, was a knuckleduster which locked in place to form a butt for a six-shot revolver, whilst a folding blade converted the weapon into a dagger.*

Bottom: *designed to be concealed in the palm of the hand, this form of revolver was known as a 'Protector' and was patented in the USA in 1883 by a Frenchman Jacques Turbiaux. To load, the side plate was unscrewed to reveal a disc cut to hold the cartridges. To fire, the barrel was projected between the fingers and the trigger bar was pressed home with the palm*

sisted of a small, six-shot revolver, rather like a small pepperbox and attached to the side of the frame was a short dagger blade which could be swung forward and locked into position. To complete this three purpose weapon there was a knuckleduster fitted at the rear of the cylinder and so fixed that it could be clipped back to serve as a butt for the revolver or, folded down under the cylinder, serve its usual function, its effect enhanced by the weight of the cylinder grasped in the fist.

However, the prize for initiative in this field must surely go to a Walter Davies who, in 1877, patented the ultimate in combination weapons. His patent provided for a military sword fitted with a revolver but the touch of genius was provided by making the scabbard collapsible so that it could be folded up to make a shoulder stock converting the weapon into a carbine.

Concealed guns. Most combination weapons were obvious with little or no attempt to disguise their true nature but this was not always so and firearms have been hidden in locks, whips, and keys, to mention but a few of the odd containers. Walking-stick guns have always been popular with poachers for with a press and a turn, a chamber for a 410 cartridge is revealed. These weapons are nothing new for sticks concealing pistols back to the early days of firearms and wheel-lock and flintlock versions are known. Percussion versions are quite common and in most the body of the cane forms the barrel of the gun, the muzzle being protected by a wooden or cork ferrule.

Pistols for the horse rider have been concealed in the handle of whips whilst for the pessimist who feared attack on a rainy day a few were fitted into the handle of umbrellas. Even the sturdy pipe smoker was not forgotten and small pistols, usually firing a .22 cartridge, were cleverly disguised as pipes, either in the style of a simple briar or a less conventional type. Ladies were not neglected and ingenious purses were made with a pistol, often of the pepperbox type, concealed in one of the compartments. For the Japanese Samuari Lord there were pistols concealed in false fans and these, as with almost everything Japanese, were beautifully and tastefully decorated. The demands of partisan and underground warfare revived interest in concealed weapons and during the Second World War some ingenious but highly

A pocket-knife pistol. A simple barrel, 1.4 inches long, was cut to take a small pin fire cartridge which was fired by the long bar hammer. On cocking the hammer, the concealed trigger clicked down into position ready for firing. The barrel is stamped 'D.R.P. 2', German, late 19th century. Overall length with blades closed – 3 inches

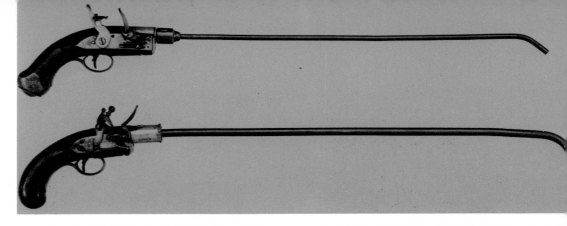

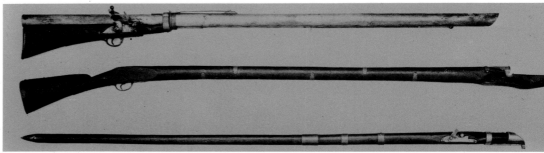

lethal devices were designed including some that fired, not bullets, but poisoned darts.

Rather than disguise a pistol many inventors patented ideas for weapons which could be concealed and fired conveniently in one hand. The commonest variety is probably the 'Protector' revolver which consisted of a circular block of metal cut to hold a number of small-calibre cartridges. This disc was housed in a circular metal frame from the side of which projected a short barrel whilst on the opposite side was a bar which operated the firing pin. Protectors were held in the palm of the hand with the fingers clenched and the barrel projecting between the first two fingers. Squeezing the hand forced the rear bar home to fire the first shot, unclenching the hand allowed the internal mechanism to rotate the turret bringing the next cartridge into position.

Another small 'palm' pistol was that patented by James Reid of New York in 1865. Again it was basically a small pepperbox revolver designed to fit easily into a pocket or purse, but its unusual feature was its flat, all metal butt which was pierced by a large hole. If it was intended only to thump an assailant rather than shoot him, the body of the weapon was held in the palm of the hand and the little finger slipped through the hole in the butt which left a section of the metal butt projecting ready to administer some very hefty blows.

Timepieces and alarms. Firing systems were pressed into service for various purposes such as alarms, traps, and timing devices. Probably the simplest of all was the sundial timer which was made up of a small barrel holding a charge of powder. From the touch-hole, a train of powder was laid and mounted above this was a large lens which could be adjusted to focus the sun's rays. With the aid of a sundial the angle and direction of the glass could be set so that at a given time the sun's rays ignited the powder and so fired the gun. Flintlock guns were made to operate from trip lines set on the ground and such devices were popular with land owners anxious to defend their game against the intrusion of poachers.

The percussion cap, so much simpler to use, was utilised in a variety of devices, alarm guns, to warn of intruders. Basically they consisted of a very simple pistol mechanism which was set in a wedge-shaped block. If the block was set on the floor just under the edge of a door, should it be opened the bottom would ride over the wedge, activate the trigger and fire a small warning charge as well as jamming the door.

All the weapons and ingenious devices mentioned so far have been conventional in one respect for they fired normal type projectiles, but some

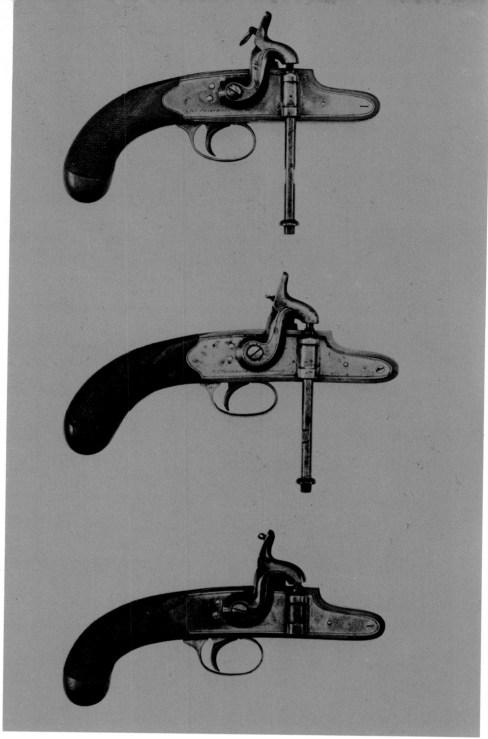

Very unusual indeed are these percussion cap testers which were designed to find out the optimum force required to detonate the cap. The tension of the mainspring could be adjusted and a wire was attached to the ring at the top of the cock and fixed to a gauge which would then register the force required for detonation. The end of the rod at the side of the body was fitted on the touch hole of the testing mortar. The testers are engraved 'R. T. PRITCHETT LONDON' on the lock. English, circa 1860

A mysterious weapon, for this is basically a typical German wheel-lock of about 1580 with large ball butt and inlay decoration. At a later date, possibly the 18th or 19th century, it has been converted to a seven barrelled 'duck-foot' gun. This type of weapon was popular with those who feared riot or mutiny where a mob might be involved, since diverging barrels were intended to spread a volley over a wide area

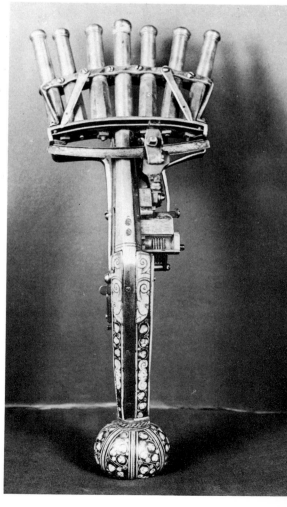

inventors rejected these for reasons best known to themselves. In 1718 a Mr James Puckle patented a repeating tripod mounted gun which could fire several shots at one loading; this in itself was perhaps not too startling but Mr Puckle made a distinction of targets. When used against fellow Christians the bullets were round but against the Turks they were to be square and special barrels were provided for use with these unique missiles. There is also at Windsor a German-made sporting gun with a barrel designed for a heart-shaped bullet.

With the advent of repeating firearms much of the stimulus for novelty weapons was removed but for sheer flamboyance and misplaced ingenuity the award must surely go to the unknown designer of a set of equipment found in France. It consisted of a cuirass adapted to hold nineteen pistols which protruded from the front like a hedgehog's quills. To load, the pistols were dropped forward and the cartridges inserted; the pistols were then returned to the firing position from whence they could be fired in groups of four or five by operating a series of studs. Accompanying this marvel of complication were a pair of stirrups each containing two pistols fired by pulling on a strap! It would be very difficult to follow such an invention.

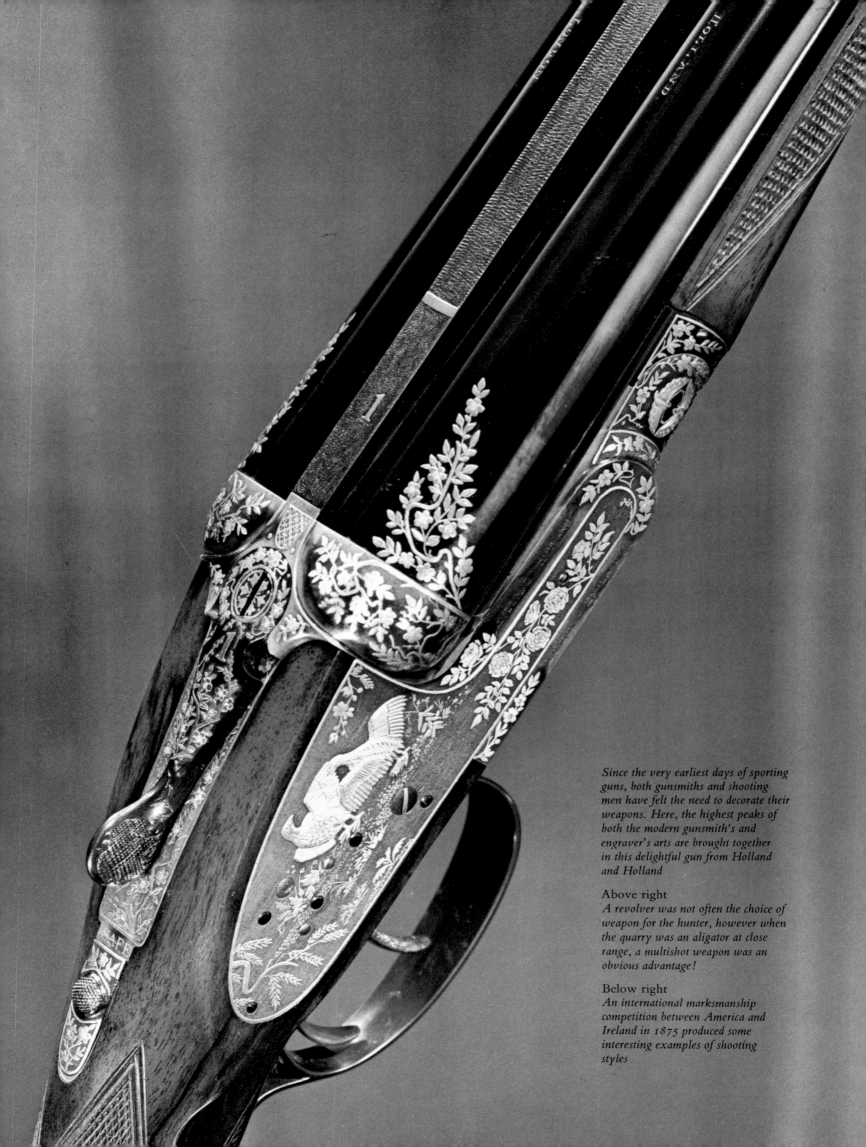

Since the very earliest days of sporting guns, both gunsmiths and shooting men have felt the need to decorate their weapons. Here, the highest peaks of both the modern gunsmith's and engraver's arts are brought together in this delightful gun from Holland and Holland

Above right
A revolver was not often the choice of weapon for the hunter, however when the quarry was an aligator at close range, a multishot weapon was an obvious advantage!

Below right
An international marksmanship competition between America and Ireland in 1875 produced some interesting examples of shooting styles

CHAPTER IV

HUNTING AND SPORTING GUNS

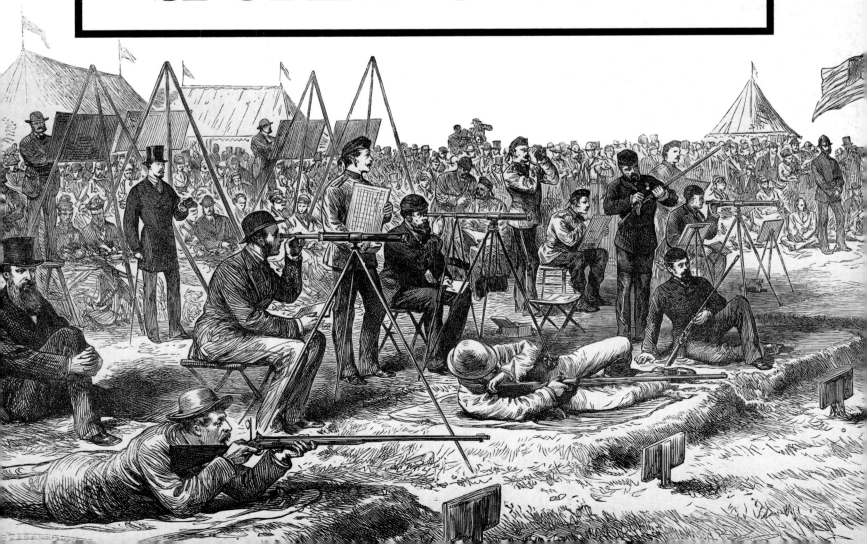

nce upon a time, long, long ago, there was only one type of gun. Then, someone had the bright idea of making spiral grooves inside the barrel and then there were two types of gun, the smooth bore shotgun and the rifle. From that day forward, the number of types of gun has proliferated to the delight of the gun enthusiast and the despair of the ammunition maker.

A great many people who are skilled and competent users of firearms only have one gun, others might have a shotgun and a rifle and if called upon to justify their attitude, can do so with complete sincerity and considerable justification. Other people have a whole armoury of guns most of which are rarely used and in fact, this sort of person is really a gun collector rather than a gun user.

Somewhere between the two extremes lies an acceptable compromise; a compromise between the idea of a gun as a mere tool and the idea of a gun as an expensive decoration – a conversation piece which the owner would be reluctant to take out in the rain in case the stock became damaged. An understanding of the history and development of sporting guns can increase the pleasure and satisfaction of both ownership and use in the field, and, although the development of the shotgun and the rifle are not exactly parallel, for our purposes we can talk about both since both are used for sporting purposes.

Early shotguns. Smoothbore guns were used for fowling during the 16th and much of the 17th Centuries. The common mode of use at that time being in conjunction with a stalking horse. One of the earliest works in English which refers to shooting was the classic treatise by Gervase Markham, *Hunger's Prevention or the Whole Art of Fowling*. Trees and bushes made from painted canvas could also be used if the natural cover was insufficient. The taking of both land and waterfowl during this period was not so much a sport or pastime but more of a necessary means of augmenting a winter diet lacking in meat.

An 18th Century flintlock single barrel gun by Florkin, Liège, a fine example of a European quality firearm

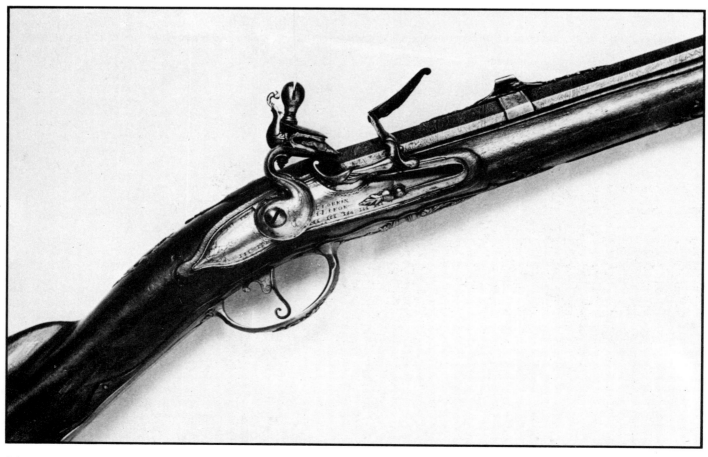

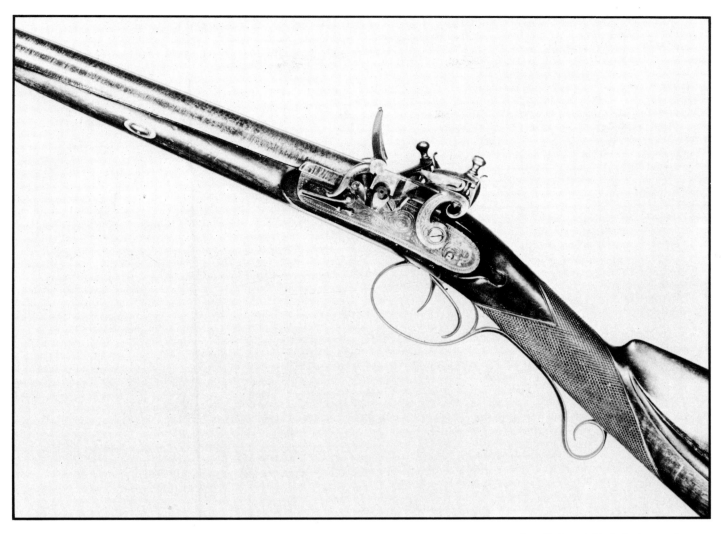

Double barrel flintlock shotgun by John Manton, Dover Street, London. Fitted with vertical sears, and rounded dove-tailed pan. Circa 1825, the final and perfected design of flintlock

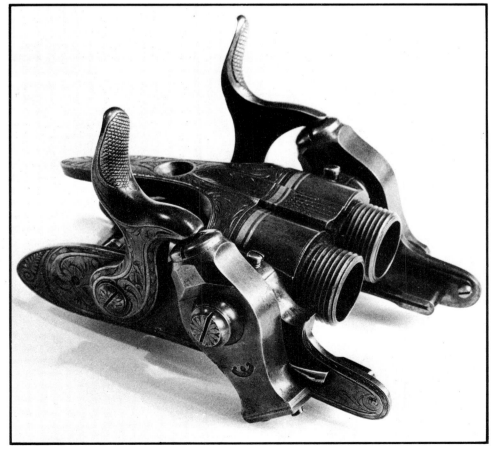

Breeching for a double gun with Forsyth & Co's roller primer locks, more commonly known as 'scent bottle' locks

English flintlock sporting rifle with damascus barrel and lock by Griffin, circa 1740. The stock is of walnut with brass mounts and bears the arms of John, 4th Lord Carmichael and 3rd Earl of Hyndford (born 1701, died 1767)

The main method of taking game was by the use of nets, snares, decoys, and bird lime. When firearms were employed the birds were shot on the ground and not flying so there was little incentive to improve the handling qualities of the weapon. Nevertheless, even from these early days sporting weapons were not merely considered to be tools of the chase, for in 1604, James I sent Philip II of Spain 'Foure fowling pieces with there furniture, very richly garnished and inlaid with plates of gold'. Throughout the entire history of firearms quality weapons have been employed to cement friendships between princes although it has to be admitted that such prestige arms were works of art rather than weapons of utility.

Proportionately, a greater number of sporting rifles appear to have survived the ravages of the years, and there is little doubt that the tradition which accords the credit for the invention of the rifled barrel to Germany is correct. It would, of course, be rather nice to be able to state with accuracy when, where, and by whom! Nevertheless we know that rifle guns were used in Germany for sport, mainly deerstalking, and for markmanship competitions as many of our larger museums are fortunate to have examples of wheel-lock hunting rifles of the 16th and 17th centuries.

Such weapons as have survived from this early period serve to illustrate the taste of the noble and wealthy sportsman since the wood stocks are embellished with either inlay or marquetry of engraved stag horn, rare woods and, occasionally, ivory. On arms of the highest quality, the barrel and lock-plate could be etched and gilded or decorated by gold damascene work.

Flintlock guns. The first significant improvement in the design of sporting guns occurred with the development of the flintlock which, although it did not entirely replace the wheel-lock for many years, was made in far greater numbers and in a wide range of quality. Also, during the 17th Century, effective repeating sporting guns appeared and the noted English diarist, Samuel Pepys refers to one type in his diary for 3 June 1662, 'a gun to discharge seven times, the best of all devices I ever saw, and very serviceable, and not a bauble, for it is much approved of, and many thereof made.' Two

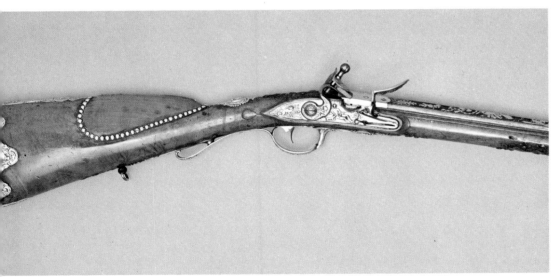

Flintlock fowling piece with lock signed 'Delety A' Paris Rue Coquilliere'. The barrel bears the stamp of Pedro Esteva, Barcelona, the silver mounts bear the Paris mark for 1770

Flintlock fowling piece by Durs Egg. A fine example of silver inlay decoration, hall-marked 1801–2

59

years later, Pepys, on 4 March 1664 saw another type of repeating weapon when he visited his friend Lord Sandwich. He relates, 'there were several people be trying a new-fashion gun brought my Lord this morning, to shoot off often, one after another, without trouble or danger, very pretty.'

There is no doubt that Samuel Pepys would be made most welcome in any sporting company today, three centuries later, for he bought one of the ingenious repeating guns himself and when he met 'one Truelocke, the famous gunsmith' in the Bull-Head Tavern, the gunsmith took his gun to pieces for him and showed him how it worked. Although the gunsmith was not entirely satisfied with the safety of the gun, Pepys himself was 'mighty satisfied with it' – a dyed in the wool gun-nut!

Ingenious minds had produced ideas for repeating flintlock weapons and a few skilled and expensive craftsmen had been able to translate these ideas into practice. A scheme of more practical utility was the use of rifled 'turn-off' or screwed barrels which permitted the charge to be introduced at the breech with a considerable improvement in accuracy and hitting power.

The 17th Century was a period of experiment and technical innovation in firearms whereas the 18th was one of refinement. The practice of shooting birds on the wing resulted in an increased demand for fine sporting guns and the typical weapon of this period was the long, single-barrelled flintlock, full-stocked to the muzzle. By 1750, a representative sporting gun would have a barrel between 36 and 46 in. long and a bore between 0.60 in. and 0.75 in.

The classic sporting gun as we know it today traces its ancestry back to the double flintlock shotgun with side-by-side barrels which first made its appearance in the second half of the 18th Century.

One of the greatest improvements was not readily apparent by casual external observation. This was Henry Nock's patent breech which appeared in 1787. The common practice of closing the breech end of the barrel was to screw in a plug and in front of this plug a hole or vent was bored through the barrel which communicated the flash from the pan to the charge in the barrel. Improved ignition of the charge had been obtained by the use of 'chamber breeching' but although such guns shot harder, the ignition time was longer, negating the care and attention lavished on the locks by the lockmaker. Nock's invention eliminated this delay and the stage was set for the introduction of the flintlock double shotgun which in the opening years of the 19th Century was to raise the art of gunmaking in Britain to a pinnacle of perfection.

Thomas B. Johnson in his *Shooters Guide or Complete Sportsman's Companion* published in 1816 gives us some idea of contemporary opinion and

Double pin-fire shotgun engraved by J. Boussart, Liège, circa 1880

illustrates the advances made. He states 'the fowling piece which I should recommend is one with a stub twisted barrel, patent breech, platina or gold touch-hole, and to the person who is in the habit of shooting below the mark, an elevated breech, the length of the barrel from 26 in. to 28 in.'. By this time mechanical improvements to the lock such as the elimination of friction by the use of roller bearings and link swivels helped to increase the speed of ignition. This factor coupled with the greater care and attention that was paid to the mechanism also improved the certainty of ignition. The result of both improvements was a weapon which proved to be of greater satisfaction to the sportsman of the time.

Amongst a list of the top makers in Johnson's book is found the name of Manton. What is not clear from the book is that there were two Mantons. John Manton born in 1752 and Joseph, his younger brother, born in 1766: John worked for the famous London maker Twigg of Piccadilly and before setting up on his own account in 1781 had risen to the position of foreman. John Manton had his younger brother Joseph as an apprentice until he left in 1789 to start up his own business. The effect that the two Mantons had on the design and manufacture of sporting guns cannot be over-emphasised. This is best

This is the Fusilier Model of 1860, one of the many military versions of the famous Prussian Needle Gun, first adopted in 1841. The first true ancestor of our modern bolt action sporting gun

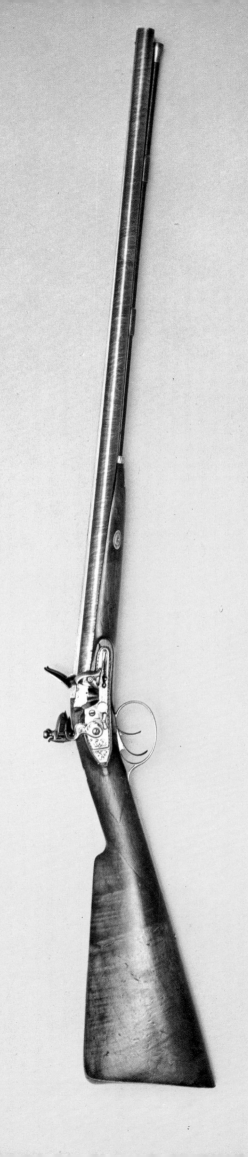

A fine example of the work of one of the great names in the development of the sporting gun. A double flintlock shotgun by Joseph Manton, circa 1815

Double barrelled percussion shotgun by Westley Richards, circa 1845

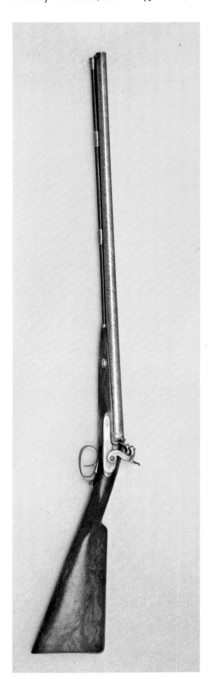

62

illustrated by comparing a Manton gun with one by a provincial maker, there is an elegance of line, an attention to the minutest detail which is unmistakeable. Pick up the Manton and you will discover that its qualities are such that the sportsman of today is quite likely to say, 'you know – I think I could shoot really well with that gun'.

Detonating guns. The 19th Century not only saw a revolution in the art and craft of gunmaking. Another revolution of a far more fundamental kind took place in the opening years of the century; the invention of the detonating gun. Far away from the centres of gunmaking a Scottish clergyman, the Rev. Alexander Forsyth, had been experimenting with fulminating compounds at his Manse at Belhelvie in the north of Scotland. Forsyth's story has been told and re-told too often to justify repetition here, but guns built on his principle, which eliminated the tyranny of flint and steel, were built in London by James Purdey. Purdey had worked for Joseph Manton and he established his own business, which was to gain world-wide recognition, in 1814. Forsyth formed his own company in June 1808 and the firm continued in business until 1852. The original detonating system based on the Forsyth 'scent-bottle' lock was replaced by a system based on a copper cap, the inventor of which is unknown.

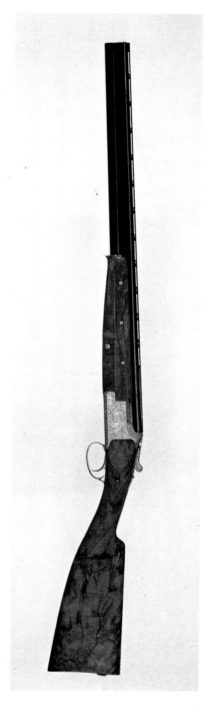

Top quality Browning FN over and under shotgun. This is FN's top quality game model with the company's D5 engraving

Colonel Hawker, author of *Instructions to Young Sportsmen* rather coyly mentions that he had suggested the idea of a copper cap to Joseph Manton and the famous Joseph Egg described himself on his guncase labels as the 'Inventor of the Percussion Cap' and many others advanced claims or had claims advanced for them. It is unlikely that we shall now with any degree of certainty who was responsible, but whoever it was is commemorated every time a gun is fired for even today the cartridge is ignited by a copper cap in the base of the case.

The percussion shotgun became an instrument of perfection and a delight to use. Its performance on the pattern plate and in the field left little to be desired and one of the most pleasant guns to use in my own modest collection is a 17 bore double percussion gun by William Greener of Birmingham.

The rifle cannot be considered to have achieved the same standard of perfection at this time as the invention of the percussion cap cannot be said to have improved accuracy. Neither did its advent significantly increase the speed of loading. The problem with the muzzle-loading rifle was to get the bullet to 'take' the rifling and many were the schemes – some ingenious, some brutally crude – which were thought up to achieve this end. Accuracy could be obtained if considerable care was taken in loading.

However, by the mid 19th Century the muzzle-loader gave way to the breechloader and it was the Military who led the way. In America, Britain, and Europe, conversion breeches were screwed on to the sawn-off breech end of muzzle-loading rifles. These were followed by true cartridge breech-loaders employing one or another of the 'block' actions.

Of the block actions, perhaps the most widely used was the Martini, developed from the American Peabody action. This was adopted by Britain as the Martini-Henry service rifle and used by generations of riflemen in rim-fire calibres for both sporting and target use and also as an inexpensive shotgun.

Of the numerous block actions which appeared in the second half of the 19th Century, the Heeren has survived, but of even greater interest has been the revival quite recently of this type of single shot action typified by the American Ruger falling block series of rifles. Many of these falling block rifles such as the Farquharson and the Henry have been rescued from the gun collector's gun rack and brought back into useful life by rebarreling to a modern calibre, but the Ruger is the first attempt to produce this type of rifle by modern production methods.

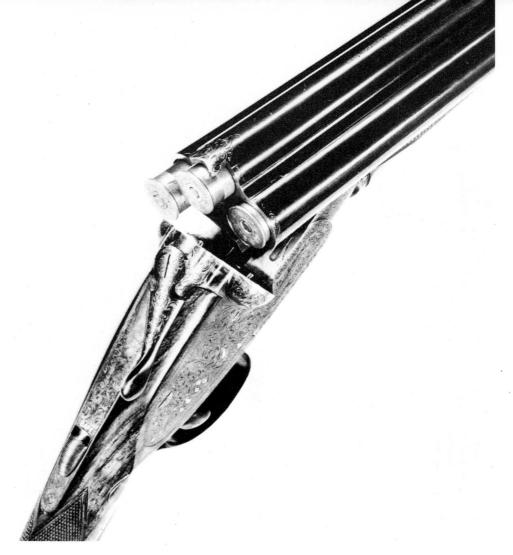

An unusual Westley-Richards three barrel shotgun made in 1911 to Green patents. Single trigger, selective ejector. All three barrels 16 bore

Bolt action guns. Of all the types of rifle which have been used for sporting purposes, there is little doubt that the most widely used is the bolt action. The first effective bolt action rifle was the Dreyse *Zundnadelgewehr* of 1838. This was the first production rifle in which the breech was closed by a sliding and turning bolt similar in principle to the common door bolt and it is to be wondered that this idea was not employed at an earlier stage. The reason is that at this early stage of development, a satisfactory cartridge capable of sealing the breech had not yet appeared. The Dreyse Needle Gun employed a very odd cartridge, which although it contained projectile, propellant *and* the means of ignition, lacked any means of sealing the breech. The escape of gas from the breech when the Needle Gun was fired resulted in the Prussian infantry firing from the hip rather than from the shoulder! Nevertheless, in spite of this and other problems, the Dreyse gun prooved to be a most formidable military arm and not only did it unite the German Empire but it also rendered obsolete the muzzle-loading military rifles of Europe.

The Needle Gun led the way for the introduction of the Mauser rifle, the first practical design of which was patented in the names of an American, Samuel Norris, an agent for the Remington Arms Company, and Wilhelm and Peter Mauser of Oberndorf, Württemberg, Germany. Norris enters the picture but briefly, the legitimate inventors being the brothers Mauser. It was Peter who developed every good feature of the modern metallic cartridge turning bolt action and he did the job so well that the Mauser rifles and Mauser type rifles developed from the Belgian Model Mauser rifle adopted by the Belgian Government in 1889 are fundamentally similar. However, we are moving ahead in time just a little too quickly! Important developments of the rifle had come from Germany and it is to France that we must look to find what was happening with shotguns. At the beginning of the second half of the 19th Century the muzzle loading shotgun was at the height of its development and if we disregard the time taken to reload, it was a highly efficient and very handsome firearm.

When the breech of the Darne gun is closed, the fine lines of a high class gun are revealed. This gun is decorated with particulary attractive engraving

Although the muzzle loader was an improvement on the flintlock, there was still the need to measure out the correct charge of black powder for each barrel. This was easily and quickly done (using a special powder flask having a graduated measure) but care had to be taken to ensure that two charges were not put down the same barrel, not as difficult as might be thought if the birds were coming thick and fast. Wads followed the powder and shot was then introduced (again from a special flask which had provision for measuring out the correct charge). Over-shot wads were then rammed down on top of the shot and the nipples or pivots capped with copper detonating caps.

The breechloading cartridge. It was the introduction of the breech-loading selfcontained cartridge which was to greatly simplify the whole operation of loading. In Britain the first indication of the coming revolution was given at the famous Great Exhibition of 1851, where the Lefaucheaux or 'French crutch gun' as it was known, was displayed. This gun was fitted with hinged drop down barrels and was adapted for use with the pin-fire cartridge. This cartridge had been developed by the Frenchman Houillier and patented by him in 1846. Initially, trouble was encountered with split cases and instances of weak shooting but the pin-fire was the first successful breechloading cartridge and enjoyed a surprisingly long life, in fact, one or two European firms still load pin-fire cases.

The pin-fire was not the only contender in the breechloading stakes, for a cartridge not unlike the Dreyse Needle-Gun cartridge had been introduced for shotguns by Joseph Needham and needle-fire shotguns were made both by Rigby of Dublin and Joseph Needham. The Needham gun enjoyed a period of brief popularity, one owner stating that he would be 'greatly surprised to find anyone who gave it (the Needham) a fair trial ever using another description of field piece'. In its favour the advocates of the needle-fire system put forward the benefits of cheaper cartridges (half the cost of the pin-fire), ease of manufacture (the sportsman could easily make them himself), and ease of use in the field since there was not the bother and difficulty of extracting the fired cases, the thin paper case went up the barrel with wad and shot!

Although the eminent Birmingham gunmaker William Greener had said that 'no fear need be entertained that the use of breechloaders will become general', this rather sweeping statement proved to be quite false and the number of breechloading systems began to proliferate. Charles Lancaster introduced his central-fire shotgun which was built on much improved lines to the earlier Lefaucheaux. This was followed by a central-fire breechloader by G. H. Daw which employed a cartridge based on French patents essentially similar to those used today. Improvements in the lockwork followed and the introduction of the double rotary underlever provided one of the strongest breech closures ever employed.

By the 1860s the muzzle loader, although still used, was in retreat and British gunmakers were engaged in perfecting the breechloading shotgun for the Victorian sportsman, a man with an unrivalled purchasing power and endowed with critical faculties. The London and provincial makers vied with each other for a share in this lucrative market and in so doing established a reputation which even today stands them in good stead. The early breech-loader had to be closed by hand, Purdey introduced his snap action, originally with a short lever in the front of the trigger guard, and later to be operated by a top lever, still the most widely used and satisfactory method of breech closure. Rebounding locks which eliminated the need to draw back the external hammers to half-cock were introduced and for many, the top lever non-ejector with rebounding locks is still regarded as one of the most elegant shotguns ever made. Do not for a moment think that all such guns are in museums; a surprising number are still in use, a century after they left the gun-maker's shop.

Hammerless and ejector guns. Two tiresome jobs had still to be carried out by the sportsman, he had to cock the hammers and he also had to remove the fired cases. The 1870s saw the appearance of a number of 'hammerless' guns. To be more precise most were *internal* hammer guns where the internal hammers were cocked when the lever was operated to open the gun. To cock two hammers with a short lever meant that the sportsman had to have quite a strong thumb. To help overcome this problem a longer lever was employed – the gunbarrels themselves.

The first hammerless gun which employed the fall of the barrels themselves to cock the hammers was the famous Anson & Deeley. This was not a development or improvement on a previous design, it was a radical development which is still the basis of many side-by-side double shotguns made throughout the world to this day. First of all, the number of components in the lockwork were drastically reduced. There were only three main limbs in each lock and although the early Anson & Deeley guns made by Westley-Richards employed the Westley-Richards 'doll's head' extension to bolt and barrels, later versions employed the Purdey bolt, either alone or in conjunction with the doll's head extension.

Once barrel cocking had been established, similar systems were adopted for the sidelock guns which as opposed to the A & D 'boxlocks' have always enjoyed a slight superiority even if it was just snob value. The physical difference between the two types of lock lies in the mounting of the mechanism. On the former it is mounted on the lock plates let into the side of the action; on the boxlock, which Anson & Deeley first introduced in 1875, the mechanism is housed inside the action body.

Extraction systems to partially withdraw the cases from the breech when the gun was opened had been in use for some time when another development appeared – the selective ejector. The term 'selective'' is important since only the fired case had to be ejected from the gun. Systems which achieved this without unduly increasing the weight, bulk or difficulty of operating the gun and which had a truly remarkable degree of reliability appeared and were accepted.

Lastly, the traditional double gun with side-by-side barrels was to benefit from one more improvement, the single trigger. Here again, the amount of ingenuity expended on the development of the various systems which finally gained the approval of sportsmen was truly remarkable and anyone who has examined the patent literature on the subject would have thought that all possible systems had been examined long ago. This is not the case for as recently as 1962, a new idea was patented by Fausto Massi, gunmaker of Vicenza in Northern Italy.

One of the advantages of the double shotgun is the ability to select immediately the right degree of choke and consequently the appropriate shot pattern for the range and target. This is possible, since, traditionally the degree of choke in each barrel differs. With a non-selective single trigger mechanism, the right barrel is fired first; with a selective mechanism, the selector has to be moved if the left barrel has to be fired first. In the system proposed by Fausto Massi, the front trigger fired the right and then the left barrel. If it is wished

Nearly a century after the introduction of the famous Winchester Model 1873, Winchester still make the popular lever action. This is the Model 88 available in .243, .284, and .308 Winchester calibres

to fire the left barrel first, the finger is moved to the rear trigger. It is an interesting idea and illustrates the fact that there are still ingenious men capable of a fresh approach to problems when one might confidently expect that all approaches and solutions had long since been examined.

The basic FN Mauser rifle. Models may be dated 1924, 1924/30, 1935, etc., and calibres can be 7 mm, 7.65 mm, or 7.9 mm

Automatic rifles. Much of the development work carried out on the shot-gun up to this period was directed at increasing its rate of fire. This was also the goal of many of the rifle manufacturers of the time. The introduction of machine tools which could turn out components to a fine degree of accuracy and in large quantities was to allow the next advance to be made towards the ultimate goal of a fully automatic rifle.

America was the first country to make full use of these new manufacturing techniques with the consequence that she quickly established a lead in the production of automatic and semi-automatic weapons.

The first requirement for a rifle which, by one squeeze of the trigger, would fire, eject, reload, and recock, was a thoroughly efficient means of storing and transporting the ammunition which such a gun would consume if used to its full potential. One of the reasons why examples of flintlock guns using some sort of magazine system are so rarely seen, is the difficulty encountered in the manufacture, by hand, of such a necessarily complicated piece of mechanism.

The advent of the breechloading cartidge both in its early form which employed black powder and the more modern type using smokeless powder as the propellant, was another vital contributory factor towards the evolution of the fully automatic gun.

Gunmakers from the famous European centres such as Birmingham, Liege, St Etienne, Suhl, and Gardone, were quick to appreciate the advantages of mass production and were soon seeking knowledge of the new techniques in America. It was not very long before the machine tools were brought to Europe for the new gun factories which were soon to replace the hundreds of small workshops which had hitherto been the major source of production.

The American Spencer of 1860 was the first successful lever action repeating rifle. The magazine was in the buttstock and the semi-circular breechblock

Browning Automatic sporting rifle

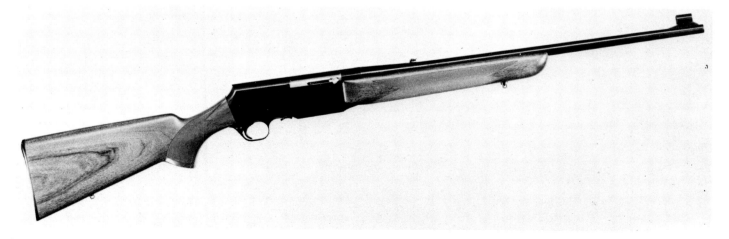

which was actuated by the trigger-guard lever had both a falling and rotary motion. Next, came the Henry of 1860, developed from the earlier Smith & Wesson and Volcanic rifles and which was later to become the Winchester, a name almost synonymous with repeating rifle.

The centre-fire Winchester Model '73 was essentially the same as the earlier Model 1866 and the Henry. Cartridges were contained in a tubular magazine under the barrel. When the finger lever was operated the breechbolt was carried to the rear and a cartridge raised by the cartridge carrier block was ready to be moved forward into the chamber by the forward movement of the breech block as the finger lever was returned to its 'rest' position. This operation also cocked the external hammer and, after firing, as the lever was again worked, the fired case was extracted from the chamber and ejected from the action.

The Winchester was subsequently further developed by John M. Browning and established a tradition in American firearms upheld by designs by Marlin in 1881 and the first hammerless lever action rifle to achieve widespread

Detail of the fine decoration on the lock plates of the Browning game model. Even the screw heads receive the attention of the engraver

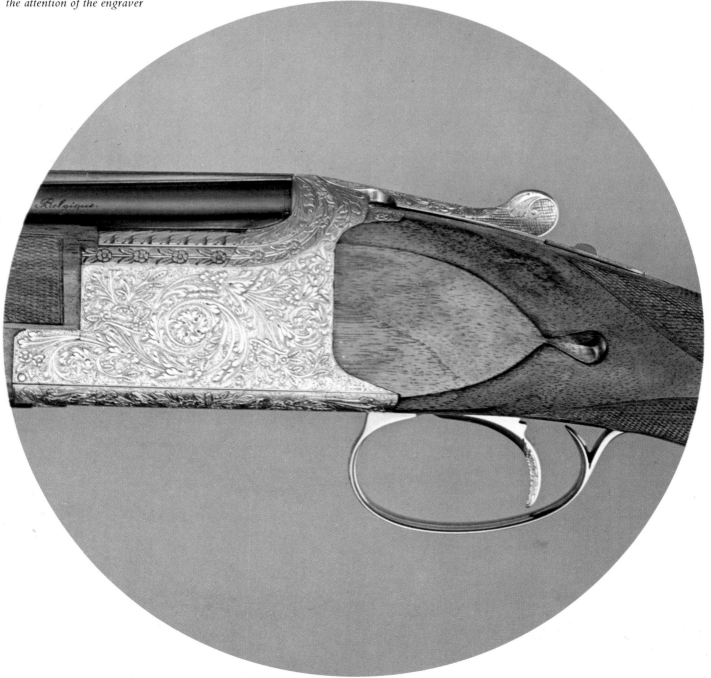

adoption, the Savage of 1899. Yet another American development was the slide action or trombone which although patented in both Britain and France was first made a practical success in America.

Meanwhile, in Europe, events had not stood still, the Belgian Mauser rifle was the first Mauser to employ a box magazine and it was the first charger loading system which permitted five cartridges to be stripped from a metal charger into the magazine, considerably speeding up reloading and yet permitting single cartridges to be introduced if necessary. An alternative to this system was invented by Mannlicher in which the cartridges and the metal clip were loaded into the magazine, the clip being expelled from the magazine when empty. Although it is perhaps slightly pedantic, the term charger is used if the cartridges are stripped into the magazine and clip is the term for the device employed when cartridges and container are loaded into the magazine together.

One other magazine development – that perfected by Schoenauer, has withstood the test of time. A director of the Austrian Arms Co. (now Steyr-

A unique sliding breech is one of the features of the guns produced by Etablissements Darne of Saint-Etienne. Insted of the usual hinged barrels, the breech slides back to reveal the chambers, a selective ejector is also incorporated

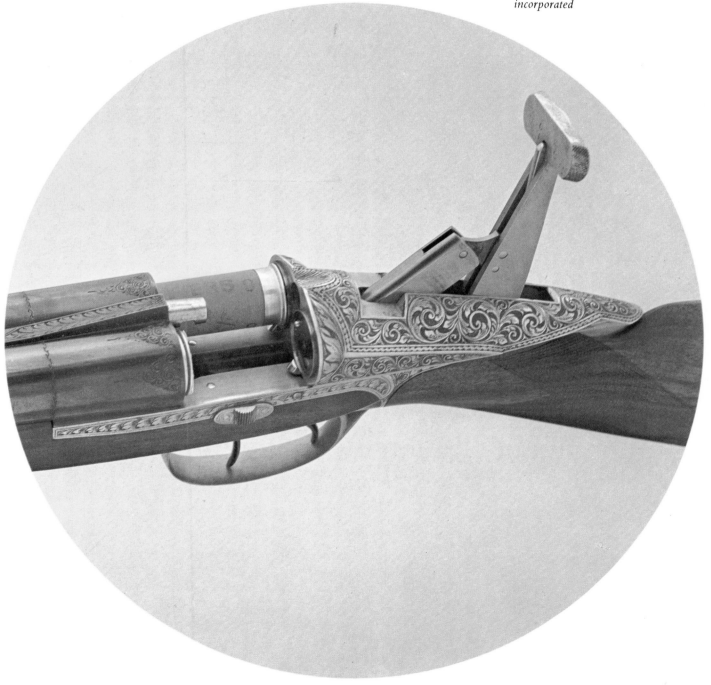

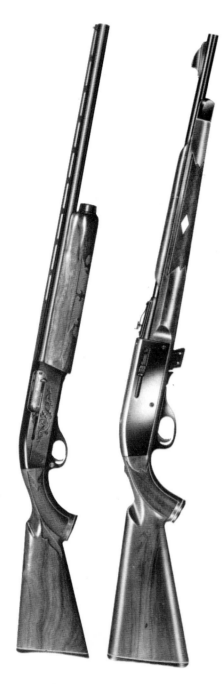

Left: *the Remington Model 1100 is a gas-operated automatic shotgun with a four shot tubular magazine. First introduced in 1963, replacing Model 58 it is available in 12, 16, and 20 gauge and 3 in. 12 gauge. Magnum, Trap and Skeet versions are to be had and barrels may be interchanged. Also available in 28 gauge and .410 as Model 1100 Small Gauge*

Right: *nylon may not be the material you associate with rifles but Nylon Zytel-101, or structural nylon, which was chosen by Remington for the original Model 66 Nylon .22 autoloading rifle has proved to be satisfactory. The Model 66 has a tubular magazine, the Nylon 77 (illustrated) uses a five shot .22 L.R. clip magazine or a ten shot clip magazine*

Daimler-Puch A.G. Austria), Schoenauer was responsible for a five-shot rotary spool magazine, which, although not the first of this type, had the neatness of a perfected design. A spool magazine is similar to the vertical box type except that instead of a magazine platform, there are a series of concave troughs arranged radially around a spindle. A coiled spring feed is used and the advantage of this design is that the cartridges are separated from one another by the radial arms of the spool. This system was of great advantage with rimmed cartridges, obviating the possibility of a jam due to the cartridge rims riding over each other. The advent of rimless cartridges did much to reduce interest in this type of magazine.

Rifles of Mannlicher design were widely used for military purposes and have been highly regarded as sporting rifles, and today not only are the products of the Steyr factory still in demand, but the English language is enriched by the term 'Mannlicher style stock' which implies a light stock with the fore-end extending to the muzzle.

A look along the rifle rack in any gun shop worthy of the name will emphasise more than anything else the predominance of Mauser type bolt-action sporting rifles. Mauser themselves manufacture a modernised version of their original action, the Model 2000 and also offer the Model 66 with a new type of action by W. Gehmann, the important feature of which is that it permits easy interchange of barrels.

For military use, the bolt action rifle has been replaced by semi-automatic weapons and there is some indication that the prejudice against self-loading rifles for sporting purposes is being slowly overcome. Certainly, in the .22 rimfire field, the bolt action is now largely supplanted by self loading autoloaders with either tubular or box magazines. In recent years, the number of auto-loading centre-fire rifles has been creeping up. Some, like the Armalite Sporter, a .223 calibre gas operated carbine, are but thinly disguised military weapons, others such as the Browning High Power Auto Rifle were designed primarily for sporting use and are available in a range of sporting calibres from .270 to .30'06. As could be expected, both Winchester and Remington offer gas-operated auto-rifles and carbines and Remington offer a slide action rifle, the Model 760, which with the Savage Model 170 are now the sole survivors of a once larger class of rifles.

Automatic shotguns. The slide action or trombone is still a very popular type of shotgun action although again it is a predominantly American type of shotgun. The Spencer shotgun was again the first successful slide action but this was overshadowed by the appearance of the Winchester series of slide action guns, the first of which, the Model 1893, was not popular, but this was followed by the improved version, the Model 1897. One of the most successful shotguns ever made, the Model 97 continued in production until 1957. Enjoying almost equal popularity was Thomas C. Johnson's Winchester Model 12. By 1943 one million had been made and even now it is in limited production although superseded by the Model 1200. Remington brought out their Model 10 in 1907. This was made under Pederson patents as was the later Model 29 which replaced the Model 10. These Remington slide action guns featured bottom ejection and are today represented by the Ithaca Model 37, still on the selling range. Remington's current slide action shotgun is the Model 870 Wingmaster.

As with the slide action, the self-loading or autoloading shotgun was of predominantly American origin. The first was the Remington Model 11 which was based on Browning's patent of 1900. This gun was introduced by Remington in 1905 and two years earlier the famous Belgian firm of Fabrique Nationale had started manufacture under Browning's patent and as the Browning Automatic Shotgun this design is still in production, a truly remarkable testimony to the rightness of Browning's original ideas. This 1900 vintage design has been more widely copied than any other, both the

Breda and Franchi autoloaders are of basic Browning design as are many others. The first new, successful change in concept occurred with the introduction, by Winchester, of their short recoil Model 50, half a century after the original Browning. Two years later, in 1956, Remington went one stage further and brought out their gas-operated Model 58, the latest version of which is the Model 1100, first introduced in 1963. Winchester also offer a gas-operated autoloader, the Model 1400.

One type of shotgun remains to be mentioned, the over and under. Once considered to be the aristocrat of shotguns when made by British firms such as Boss, Woodward, and Westley Richards, the over and under is now *the* shotgun for trap and skeet shooting and it is also found increasingly on the sporting field. Dominated today by designs derived from John M. Browning's classic over and under, still in production by Fabrique Nationale, other important designs have been manufactured notably by Beretta in Italy and by several German firms and, in more recent years, many of these designs have been copied by the gunmakers of Japan.

Many designs now half a century old are still in production and continue to give every satisfaction to the user. Many guns nearly a century old themselves are still in use and the gunmaker has always had a strong prejudice to overcome if he has been bold enough to introduce new ideas, either in method of operation or in materials of construction. There is little doubt that plastic components are to enjoy a greater degree of use in the future, the signposts being there for all to see, the Remington Nylon 66 .22 autoloading rifle and, more recently, the use of tough plastic Makrolon by the old established firm of Steyr, Diamler-Puch. This material which is used for the trigger guard and magazine of the Steyr Mannlicher rifle will not rust like steel nor scratch like aluminium and is certainly tougher than the horn which was once a favoured material for trigger guards in both Germany and Austria. Glass fibre barrels have already been tried out and providing people still have the opportunity to shoot for sport and still have the opportunity to own rifles and shotguns I think that we shall see many future developments both with regard to design and materials of construction.

Traditional methods of manufacture will continue to be patronised by those who can appreciate craftsmanship and skill and, of course, who can also

Browning over and under shotgun 'Grand Luxe' Type D4G with special engraving of the highest quality by Vrancken

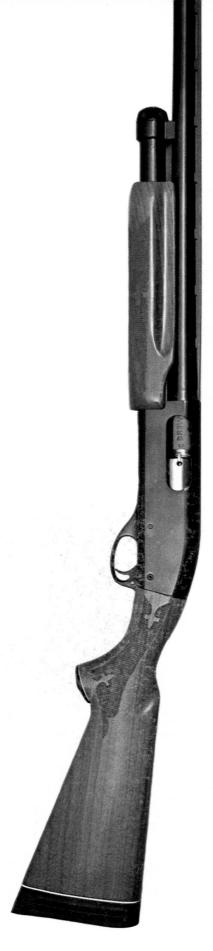

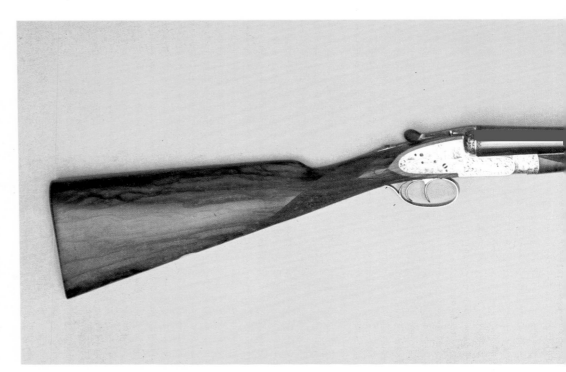

afford to pay for them. There is no doubt, however, that sporting shooting will continue to be under attack from many angles but the greatest single threat in the near future will come from the sportsman himself. The general public will, because of pressure from the mass media, demand high ethical standards and those whose attitude towards the game they pursue and to the public with whom they come in contact causes offense will have to bear the blame for the introduction of increasingly repressive measures to control and regulate sporting shooting. One of the most important single facets of our shooting is not the game which ends up in the freezer but the ethics employed in putting it there.

Gun safety. Closely allied to the question of responsibility and ethics is the overriding importance of safety. The people who make firearms and ammunition exercise considerable care to ensure that their products are fundamentally safe. In many countries, special organisations known as Proof Houses were established to guarantee, as far as possible, the safety of weapons sold in those countries. Elsewhere, sporting bodies are quick to draw the attention of their members to defective products and guidance is given by reputable gunshops jealous of their reputation. However, this is not enough, the gun owner himself has to do his part. *Accidents involving firearms do not happen, they are caused by ignorance, carelessness or stupidity.* The gun that you use should be safe and it should be kept in a safe condition and in a safe place. Carelessness can result in damage which could cause injury to the owner. Wear can cause malfunctioning which could result in an accidental discharge, which, if the gun is not pointing in a safe direction at the time, might cost someone his life. Examining the cause of fatal gun accidents, brings to light the melancholy fact that fatalities result from young people having access to firearms which, incredible though it may seem, have been left in a loaded condition. Guns and ammunition should be kept apart and should be kept in a safe and lockfast place.

Safe gun handling is not learned in a few moments, it comes with knowledge and experience and it must become automatic.

You must always treat every gun as though it were loaded – do not take anyone's word that the gun is empty, check it yourself when you accept the gun. If you do not know how to open it to verify the safe condition, return it to the owner and ask him how or leave it alone.

The Remington Wingmaster slide-action shotgun. A cartridge may be seen in the loading chamber from whence it is transported to the gun's five-shot magazine. Empty cases are ejected from a port on the under side of the gun

A modern double barrelled shotgun from Holland and Holland of London. This is the company's 12 bore 'Royal' model with standard engraving, single trigger, and 28 in. barrels

You must keep the muzzle of the gun in a safe direction. Do not point a gun at anyone. Always remember that bullets are not stopped by all walls, floors, or windows and that they can and will rocochet off growing timber, flat surfaces, and water.

You must verify your target. Bullets can go through a target and you can miss so that the bullet will go past the target – where will it end up? Make certain before you press the trigger. Use your sporting gun with caution, care and courtesy, and the men who love and respect fine firearms will respect you.

Modern double barrelled rifle by Holland and Holland, London. This is the 'Royal' model in .458 magnum calibre and has special deep carved fences. A superb example of craftmanship of the highest order

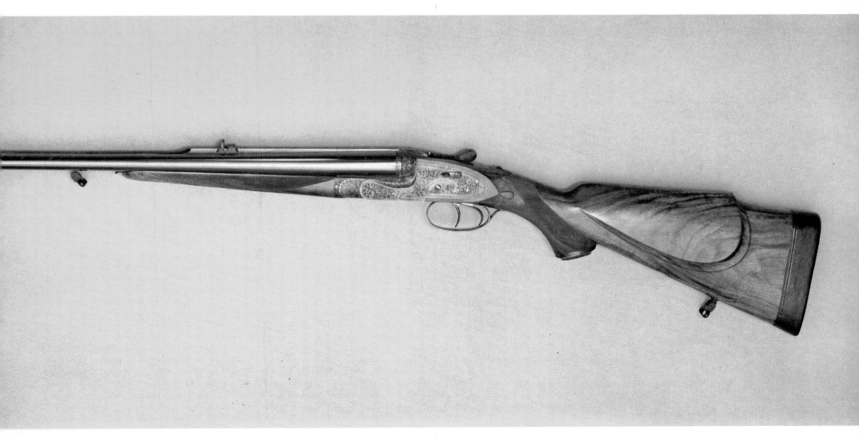

CHAPTER V

POCKET AND DUELLING PISTOLS

*A duel in France.
The weapons would
probably have been
percussion pistols
complete with rifled
barrels*

Multi-barrelled pocket pistols enjoyed a long vogue, the most popular being two superimposed barrels. The lower example, retaining the cannon-barrel design of an earlier period, dates about 1770. It and others on this system were operated by a tap on the side of the frame which directed the flash from the priming into the correct barrel. The use of short bayonets came into its own particularly on the middle quality pocket pistol after the opening decade of the 19th Century

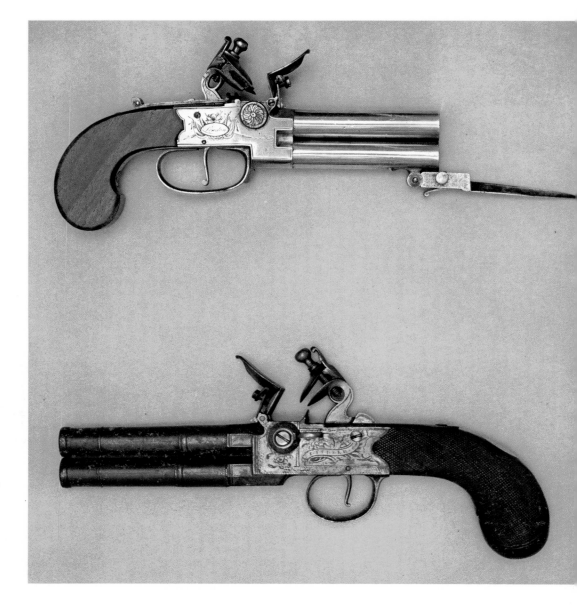

Below: a variation of the turn-off design by Ryan & Watson, about 1830. The barrel, rather than turning completely off for loading, pivots to one side to expose the breech Sheet silver and wire inlay work again became popular on some Birmingham-made pocket pistols during the 1840s and 1850s- although the quality of the work was not normally what it had been with similar decoration in the 18th Century. German silver, or plated, frames also enjoyed considerable vogue during the same years. On this example the plating of the brass frame can be seen to have worn away around the breech. The swivel ramrod was sometimes used on larger sized 'travelling pistols'

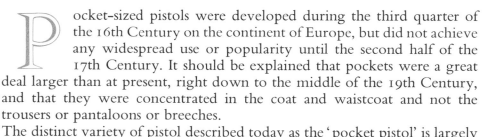

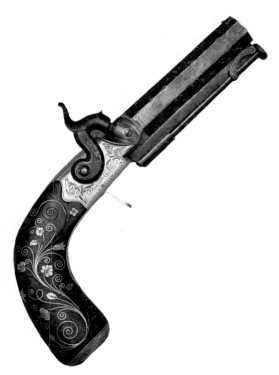

P ocket-sized pistols were developed during the third quarter of the 16th Century on the continent of Europe, but did not achieve any widespread use or popularity until the second half of the 17th Century. It should be explained that pockets were a great deal larger than at present, right down to the middle of the 19th Century, and that they were concentrated in the coat and waistcoat and not the trousers or pantaloons or breeches.

The distinct variety of pistol described today as the 'pocket pistol' is largely an English development dating from the latter part of the 17th Century and reaching its apogee a century later. There were a great many mechanical contrivances adopted to this type of pistol, mostly concerned with safety, increased firepower, and ease of use. They are also the vehicle of some fine engraving and decoration, but not on the scale lavished upon holster pistols since these little pistols were, with rare exceptions, utility pieces expected to receive long hard usage and to be seldom displayed.

The evolution of the pocket pistol. Until the 19th Century, the pocket pistol as it evolved outside of England was normally a reduced scale version of the ordinary holster pistol: a miniature. Made with side lock, half-octagonal barrel, long-spurred butt caps, and pierced sideplates, these Continental pocket pistols were so delicate in construction as almost to defy use. Far more elegant in design, and far better suited for ornamental purposes

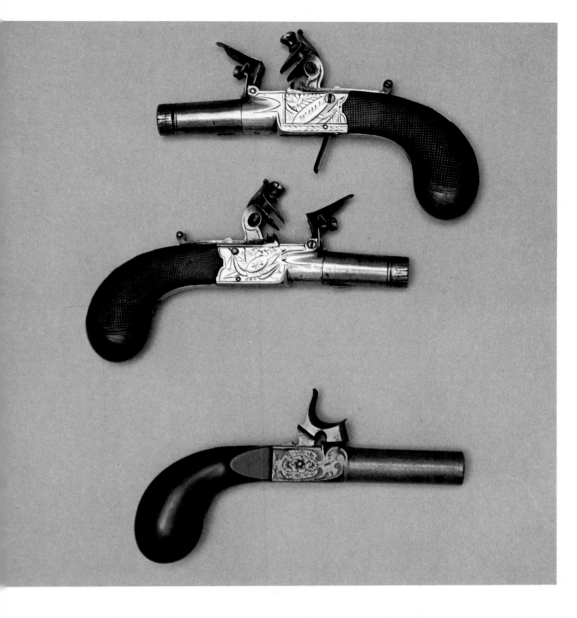

than their English contemporaries, they possessed minimum practical value.

English pocket pistols followed the Continental pattern of development in simply reducing the current design of holster pistol until the beginning of the 18th Century. The difference was that English holster pistols were generally turn-off, rifled breech loading weapons, and consequently the pocket pistol started its development in England with these special features. Some were made without trigger guards, and most used the same attractive but delicate burl walnut for stocks, which was typical of the holster pistol of the last half of the 17th Century.

The advantages of the turn-off breech loading system as applied to pocket pistols were many. Firstly, it allowed the development of maximum velocity and striking power with a minimum powder charge, for, with the ball being seated in the breech, and slightly larger than bore diameter, greatly increased pressures could be gained by the elimination of windage. No ramrod was necessary, nor any powder measure, since the chamber was simply filled to the top, and the ball rested on top of it in the semi-circular counter-sink. No patching or wadding was required, since the ball was held in position by the barrel when screwed home. Only a small spanner which fitted over a stud on the underside of the barrel was required to remove, and tighten up, the barrel.

Rifling in such small pistols, intended for short-range work only, was superfluous, and was largely discontinued by the first quarter of the 18th

Century. Normally pocket pistols were not fitted with sights, making rifling even more pointless.

By about 1700 a new design for pistols came into general use in England, which combined the metal of the breech piece with the lockplate and trigger plate. This is known today as the 'boxlock' and in its earliest form may be further described as the 'sidelock-boxlock' since the pan, steel and cock were still mounted on the right side of the pistol in the normal position. This incorporation of metalwork eliminated the fully stocked pattern, leaving only the wooden butt section. The resulting pattern came to be called the 'Queen Anne cannon-barrel turn-off pistol'. The middle of these terms refers to the fact that the round barrel was turned with rings, and reinforced to resemble the barrel of a cannon. Although described as 'Queen Anne', this type of pistol was popular until the 1760s, when a further refinement was applied to the location of the lock parts.

The Queen Anne turn-off pistol was often decorated with a cast silver buttcap in the form of a grotesque mask, and the sideplate was of pierced silver with asymmetrical scrolls and a shield. Some butts were embellished with silver wire and sheet silver inlay work. Mechanically, certain refinements were introduced, chief amongst them a safety device which locked the cock, and sometimes the cock and the steel. During this period this was generally accomplished by the trigger guard bow sliding forward and locking the parts. The steel spring was re-designed to fit underneath the pan and curve round in front of the cock, rather than to extend forward of the steel. This style of construction was applied to pistols of intermediate as well as small size, but even so it is apparent that true pocket pistols were somewhat larger in size, and less common in numbers, than subsequently. It was still an age when the power and range of the holster pistol and the strength of the belt pistol were required to meet the exigencies of self protection, and an age in which the elegancies of society did not yet require that firearms be so discreetly concealed.

With the re-location of the pan, steel, steel spring, and cock on the top of the breech section, we come to the final basic design of pocket pistol, the true boxlock. This design appeared during the 1750s, and to it were applied a great number of mechanical refinements and variations. By the 1770s it had almost entirely replaced the earlier Queen Anne style and the sidelock-boxlock mechanism. There was a diminution of size and calibre, and in common with all forms of English firearms, applied ornament suffered an eclipse in favour of blued iron furniture of plain design but high finish. Silver buttcaps did continue in use to a limited degree. Generally speaking, the numerical production of pocket pistols greatly increased during the last half of the 18th Century, and in the majority of cases there was a reduction in quality.

One of the most frequently used variations on the boxlock system was the fitting of more than one barrel. Normally this means a double-barrelled pistol of the over and under sort, but there are three-barrelled and four-barrelled versions as well. These multi-barrelled types are operated by the same mechanism located on top of the breech, but the flash of the priming is directed to each barrel in turn by the operating of a small tap on the side of the frame. By turning this small lever a cylindrical drum formed as the bottom of the pan has a differently directed touch-hole for each turning which fires the appropriate barrel when the pan has been re-primed and the mechanism readied for each shot. On multi-barrelled weapons it was not possible to utilise the same form of spanner to unscrew the barrels for loading. Notches, which closely resemble rifling grooves, were cut into the mouth of each barrel, into which fitted a square or polygonal head-key, which was used to turn off and then tighten up the individual barrels. Loading was by the same process as earlier turn-off pistols. The diminutive size and small calibre of most of these later boxlock pocket pistols was

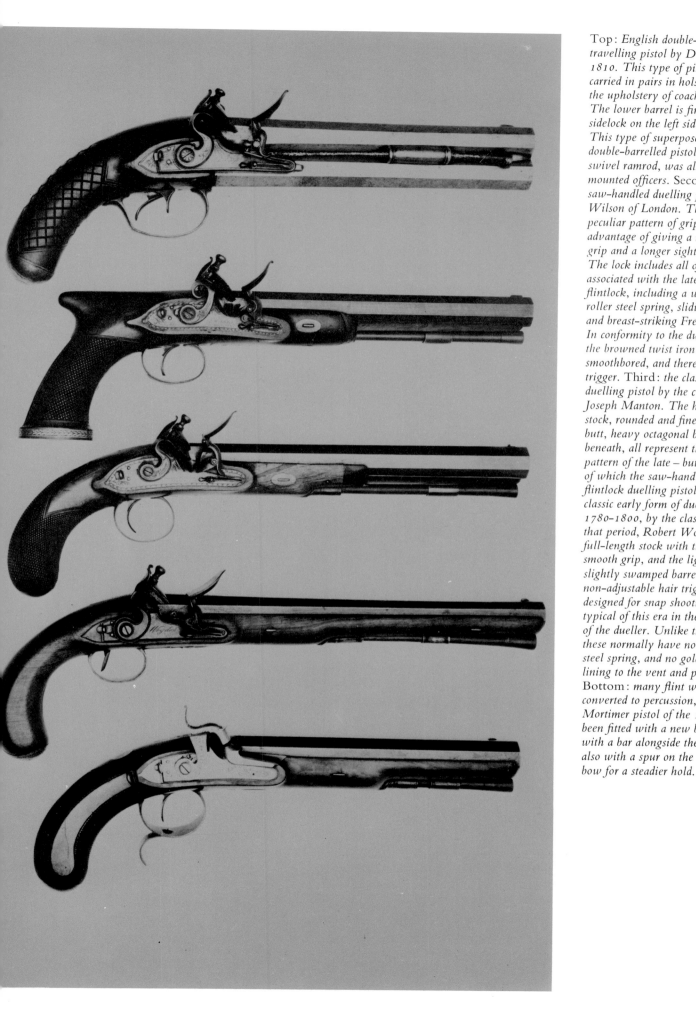

Top: *English double-barrelled travelling pistol by Durs Egg, circa 1810. This type of pistol was often carried in pairs in holsters built into the upholstery of coaches and carriages. The lower barrel is fired by a normal sidelock on the left side of the pistol. This type of superposed double-barrelled pistol, fitted with a swivel ramrod, was also popular with mounted officers.* Second: *English saw-handled duelling pistol by Alex Wilson of London. The use of the peculiar pattern of grip had the dual advantage of giving a much steadier grip and a longer sight radius. The lock includes all of the refinements associated with the late best quality flintlock, including a waterproof pan, roller steel spring, sliding safety bolt, and breast-striking French cock. In conformity to the duelling code, the browned twist iron barrel is smoothbored, and there is no hair trigger.* Third: *the classic Regency duelling pistol by the classic maker, Joseph Manton. The half-length stock, rounded and finely chequered butt, heavy octagonal barrel with rib beneath, all represent the standard pattern of the late – but not the latest, of which the saw-handle is typical – flintlock duelling pistol.* Fourth: *the classic early form of duelling pistol, 1780–1800, by the classic maker of that period, Robert Wogdon. The full-length stock with the flat-sided smooth grip, and the lightweight slightly swamped barrel, and non-adjustable hair trigger – all designed for snap shooting – are typical of this era in the development of the dueller. Unlike the later pistols, these normally have no roller to the steel spring, and no gold or platinum lining to the vent and pan.* Bottom: *many flint weapons were converted to percussion, and this Mortimer pistol of the 1790s has been fitted with a new breech plug with a bar alongside the barrel, and also with a spur on the trigger guard bow for a steadier hold.*

This pistol is unusual for many reasons: it is four-barrelled, and the barrels are of brass as well as the frame; it has provision for a ramrod which is most unusual, and is of Scottish origin

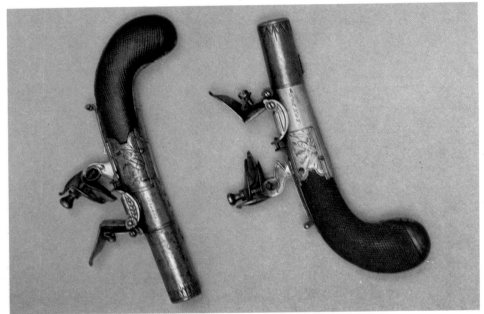

Two examples of high quality pocket pistols from the first years of the 19th Century; the brass bodied example by Henry Nock. The round frame and rounded finely chequered grip are normally the hallmark of highest quality pocket pistols, particularly during the flintlock period

partially offset as regards effectiveness by the breech loading system which allowed for greater velocity as explained earlier. Although mere pop-guns to look at, they were lethal at the short ranges for which they were intended. These small pocket pistols of the last half of the 18th Century are amongst the first pistols which were not manufactured normally in pairs, particularly those of less than first quality.

On the true boxlock pistol the breech section is normally rectangular or square in cross-section, and the corners are not rounded-off as was typical of the earlier sidelock-boxlock. By the 1780s the cannon-barrel effect was replaced with a plain round barrel. The safety catch continued to operate via the trigger guard bow on some earlier examples of the true boxlock, but the great majority of this pattern have the catch sliding along the top of the breech, just to the rear of the cock, and it is common for the better quality examples to have a stud included which locks the steel closed when the mechanism is at half-cock.

The better quality pocket pistols incorporate the refinements which were introduced on other weapons of this period such as the roller steel, and the raised pan. Another feature of design which came into use on pocket pistols several decades before appearing on the larger weapons was the ring-neck, double-throated, or throat-hole cock. This was an obvious advantage in a mechanism where the cock was stopped by a step in its breast striking the

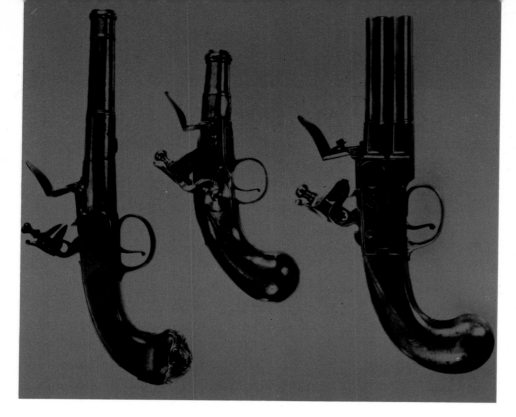

frame directly. The final improvement to appear on the boxlock pocket pistol was the concealed or spring-trigger. This feature came into general use from the 1790s, and eliminated the necessity for a trigger guard. When the cock was drawn from half to full-cock, the trigger popped out into the normal position for firing, having previously lain flush in the underside of the frame. Some flint boxlock pocket pistols have the frame rounded in cross-section, only slightly larger in diameter than the barrel, this feature being typical of the 1800-20 period on high quality examples. The butt of the majority of boxlock pistols is flat sided, with the top and bottom surfaces being flat as well; on some high quality examples the butts are rounded and finely chequered, with a silver escutcheon inlaid on the upper surface, and very occasionally with a silver lion's-head buttcap fitted.

From the middle of the 18th Century the use of the spring-bayonet became increasingly common on boxlock pocket pistols, on both single and multi-barreled types. They were commonly hinged on the underside and released by pulling back on the trigger guard bow, but many examples have the bayonet on the top, released by a catch which at first appears to be the usual sliding safety catch. More infrequently the bayonet will be hinged on the side, and released by a catch let into the side of the frame which engages the tip of the blade.

During the first years of the 19th Century the habit of making a pistol on a reduced scale but copied from a larger model came into fashion again, and

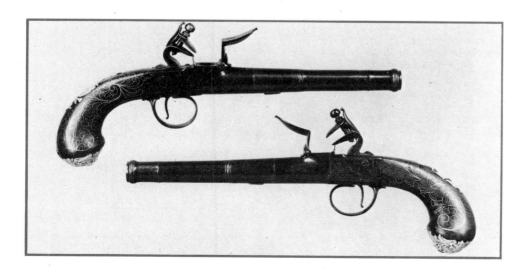

the model taken this time was the officer's pistol which was in its turn the direct descendant of the holster pistol. The small-scale pistols were normally somewhat larger than the pocket pistol, and disproportionately large in the bore, a fact which gave them the popular name of 'man-stopper', although they were more generally known as great-coat pistols. These also are often fitted with spring-bayonets, and sometimes with cannon-turned and blunderbuss-shaped barrels. While introduced during the flintlock period, they became more popular during the percussion period when the sturdy construction and simplicity of the latter system recommended it over its more fragile and complicated predecessor.

With the introduction of the percussion ignition system in the 1820s the boxlock pistol achieved far larger production, and was manufactured in vast quantities in England and Belgium, from whence it was widely exported. As a group, these later boxlock pistols represent probably the lowest level of commercial firearms production during the muzzle loading period, but there were of course best-quality exceptions to this generalization.

Undoubtedly the most famous pocket pistol of all, so far as posterity is concerned, is the 'derringer' a generic term taken from the successful publicist and large scale manufacturer of this pattern, Henry Deringer of Philadelphia. Introduced during the 1830s the derringer rapidly became a well-known companion of most American travellers during the remainder of the 19th Century. It was widely copied in America and Belgium, and with the introduction of the metallic cartridge a wide variety of single and double-barrelled types were marketed, primarily in America, all generically called derringers.

The duelling pistol. The defence of one's person became an increasingly widespread problem with the social developments of the 19th Century, and it is of interest to note that the defence of one's honour became at the same time a diminishing problem. The golden age of the Code of Honour, so far as it employed pistols and not swords as its chief instrument, was the fifty years covered by the last quarter of the 18th Century and the first quarter of

Cased pair of French duelling pistols by Boutet & Son, Versailles. Aside from the 'Empire style' of decoration, the French duelling pistol remained full stocked far longer than its English contemporary, and was normally rifled and fitted with a hair trigger. This set, plainer than most Boutet efforts, dates from circa 1818, being the end of a period in development of design begun by Boutet in the late 1780s which reached its height during the Napoleonic era. French cases normally have recessed compartments which exactly fit the piece for which they are intended

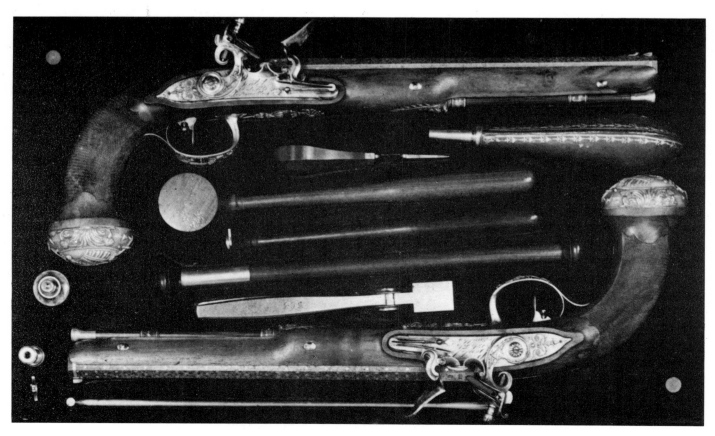

the 19th, with a continuation perhaps up to 1840. But by the close of the flintlock era public opinion was gaining a much increased hold upon the activities of the upper classes, and the study of duelling with pistols, as well as the habit, went into a decline.

The duelling pistol was a refinement of the holster pistol of the middle of the 18th Century. There is little doubt but that holster pistols were used in the early years of general acceptance of the pistol over the sword. This acceptance may be reasonably dated from the close of the Seven Years War in 1763, when the reaction against France and French customs, including the use of the sword for settling affairs of honour, set in. By the early 1770s the new pattern had been well developed. In place of the Spanish-form, or half-octagon barrel of the holster pistol, the new duelling pistol had a full octagonal barrel, of light weight and generally swamped on these early examples.

In accordance with changing fashion in gun furniture, there was little silver included on the new pistol, blued iron of relatively plain pattern taking its place. The emphasis was very strongly upon mechanical excellence and very high finish to ensure rapid ignition and accuracy. The efforts of gun makers to improve the duelling pistol in these respects were probably responsible in large part for the several basic improvements introduced to the flintlock mechanism during these years. The hair trigger, or single-set trigger, was generally adopted on these pistols. The pistol was fully stocked

Top: *cased pair of Joseph Manton duelling pistols circa 1815. There is little change in the internal design of the case, but more accessories are normally included in the later, more refined, outfits; and the case is often of oak rather than mahogany*
Below: *Boxlock percussion pocket pistols such as this were manufactured in vast quantities in Belgium, Germany and Birmingham and remained the cheapest form of personal defence firearm for most of the nineteenth century*

English box-lock turn-off pocket pistols by John Manton, circa 1790. Although of typically high quality Manton finish, these pistols represent the plain form and decoration usual on both pocket and duelling pistols of the 1790-1830 period. The green baize lined case is made so that the pistols may be carried loaded and primed, with the locks at half-cock.
The accessories include the barrel wrench (between the two pistols), ball mould, powder/ball/flints, flask, turnscrew and balls

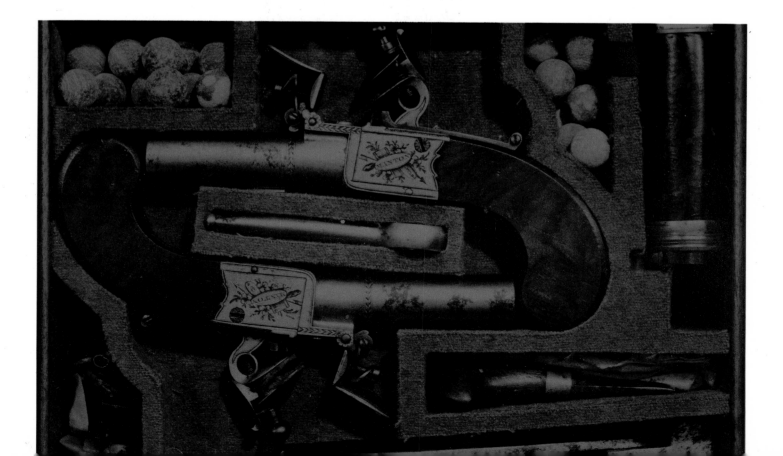

and often made especially for the hand of a particular customer – certainly in the instance of Robert Wogdon, the most famous maker of duelling pistols during the last quarter of the 18th Century.

According to the rules laid down for the functioning of the Code of Honour in England and Ireland, rifling was strictly forbidden, and the taking of deliberate aim as well: in case either was used, the indictment was for murder, and in the case of the latter, the seconds could fire upon a man taking deliberate aim. Despite this prohibition on deliberate aim, duelling pistols normally carry a foresight and a rudimentary backsight on the breech tang, presumably for determining the correct hold in practice firing. Up until the turn of the century and a bit beyond, the practice was 'snap-firing' with lightweight, hair-triggered, fully-stocked pistols. Just what caused the abrupt change in style and practice is doubtful, but change there was, both in the pistols and the method of using them.

From the lightweight, fully stocked pistol which was snap-fired, we now find developing in the first decade of the 19th Century a half-stocked pistol with a very heavy barrel, with a rib and pipes, smaller in the bore in many instances, and with a smaller and highly refined lock. These pistols normally had finely chequered grips, whereas earlier examples were usually plain. The barrels remained smoothbore, and of about the same length, viz. 10 inches, but the hair trigger was largely dropped in favour of the plain trigger with a very finely adjusted crisp pull. These pistols were intended to be pointed by both parties at the same time, firing being done on signal as

Cased pair of English duelling pistols by H.W. Mortimer, circa 1790. The design of the green baize lined mahogany case is typical; the space above the lock of the lower pistol would be for a small turnscrew. This was the case of pistols as carried to the duelling ground by one of the seconds in an affair of honour

85

nearly simultaneously as possible, or, firing in turn on the toss of a coin for first shot.

Shooting galleries cropped up to cater to a new taste for shooting at a mark with this type of pistol, and there was some caustic criticism of the practice by some gentlemen. They maintained that the original intention in getting away from the French habit of sword duelling was to put the question in the hands of fortune rather than leave almost certain victory in the hands of the best swordsman, be he right or wrong. This had been largely achieved with the earlier practice of snap-shooting with smoothbored pistols and not allowing deliberate aim. The new mode, the new heavier pistols which counterbalanced the tendency to shoot high, and the widespread practice of

The famed Kuchenreuter family
continued to produce high quality arms
during the percussion period.
This cased pair of duelling pistols is by
Bartolomaeus Joseph Kuchenreuter III
whose working life spanned the
percussion and breech-loading periods.
These pistols date from about 1850 and
illustrate the style popular at that time
throughout Germany and Austria; the
carved and chequered grip and use of
walnut as opposed to the full-fluted
grip and ebony stocks so favoured by
the French and Belgian makers

firing at wafers, developed superb marksmen with the pistol, thus reducing
the situation to what it had been with the experienced swordsman. At the
time it was generally thought that all firing at marks ought to be banned, or
persons who engaged in the habit should be set down as murderers. Nothing came of it until the whole practice of duelling was forced into abeyance
and final extinction by the growing egalitarianism of society and its mouth-
piece, the Press. It is significant that target pistols made during this period
are externally identical to the duelling pistol, but are usually rifled, fitted
with set triggers, and of smaller bore than the duelling pistol, about .45
calibre as opposed to about .50 for the dueller.

In Europe the pistol never entirely superseded the sword as the weapon

of the duel, and when pistols were used they were generally rifled. In both France and the German states there is little to tell a duelling from a target pistol in its construction. Continental pistols of this general type are often highly decorated with carved stocks, and with etched and inlaid barrels and locks. This is particularly true of best quality French and Belgian pistols. As with their English counterparts, such pistols were furnished in pairs, cased in oak, walnut, or rosewood cases, lined with baize or velvet, and fitted with a complete set of accessories for loading, firing, and cleaning. The Continental outfits are remarkable for their thoroughness in this particular, and for the ornate decoration lavished upon the accessories as well as the weapons. Duelling pistols did not receive acceptance in France until the close of the flintlock period, and the typical French weapon will be percussion.

In America the romantic sagas of single combat with a wide variety of weapons have obscured the progress and development of European style duelling and duelling pistols. Most of the latter were imported from England during the flintlock period, and even during the percussion era very few duelling pistols were actually manufactured in the United States. The Code of Honour was closely adhered to in the Southern States, but duelling went rapidly out of fashion from the beginning of the 19th Century in the remainder of the states very largely as the result of outraged public opinion when Alexander Hamilton was mortally wounded in a duel with Aaron Burr in 1804. Although individual instances of properly conducted duels are recorded after the American Civil War ended in 1865, the practice in America received its death blow at the same time as the Confederate States

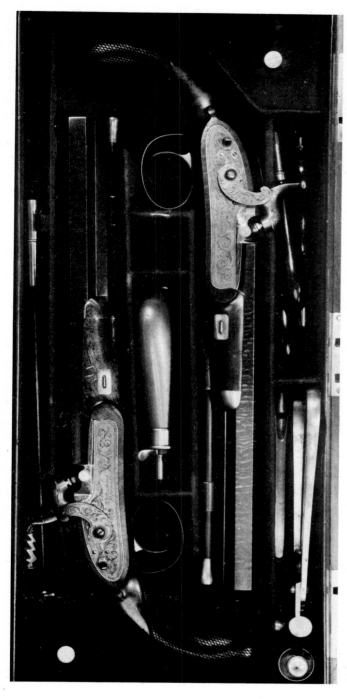

Cased pair of percussion duelling pistols by T.J. Mortimer, circa 1825. The design of the flintlock pistol is still evident – in fact except for the locks and bars on the breeches of the barrels they are virtually identical to the cased Manton pistols (opposite) circa 1815 which are also illustrated. The loading practice of the late flintlock and percussion period required a stout loading rod to force the tightly-fitting patched ball down the barrel – which still remained smoothbore. Note the spare nipple screwed into the base of nipple key in the lower right compartment

Cased pair of percussion target pistols by Charles Moore, circa 1830. Omission of the barrel rib and ramrod became a standard feature of percussion target pistols, which were always furnished with a case and complete loading accessories – including a leather faced mallet for tapping the patched ball down the bore. Note also the patch cutter. Although then known generally as the 'Westley Richards' lock' this form of lock completely surrounded by wood (the wood-bar) was apparently introduced by Charles Moore in 1827, and is probably of Continental origin. It is to this feature that the lock marking on many Moore weapons, 'Charles Moore PATENT' refers – although he did not patent the idea

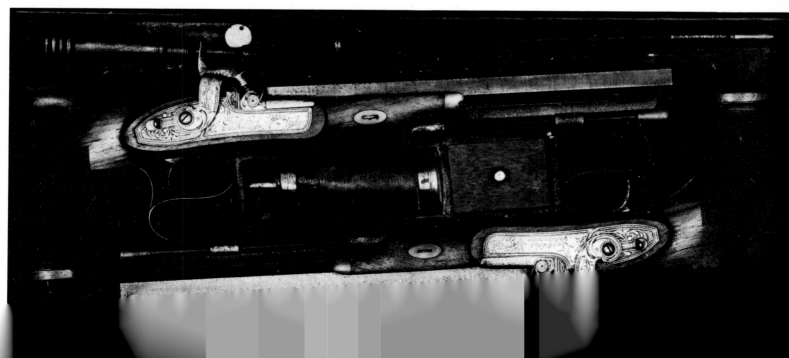

and the Europeanized society of the Old South.

The single-shot pistol lost much of its popularity to the revolver, and later to the automatic pistol: the desiderata of firepower even in pocket weapons becoming paramount in the last half of the 19th Century. The single-shot weapon has remained primarily in the form of the target pistol.

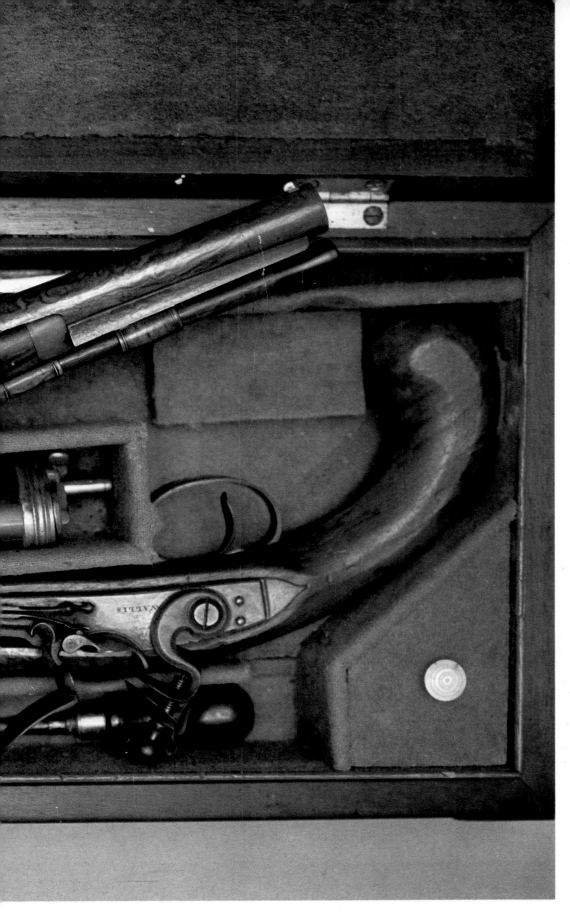

The extremely plain nature of the
English duelling pistol is here clearly
evident. Made during the 1780s, they
probably were fully stocked to the
muzzle originally, but have been
shortened and a rib fitted to conform
with the later more 'modern' style
which came in after 1800. The green
baize lining is also typical of the
English flintlock duelling pistol outfit,
as are the basic necessities in the case:
bullet mould, powder flask, turnscrew
and a loading/cleaning rod which is
missing here. The legend in which
silver furniture and other ornate
decoration typical of earlier pistols was
done away with on duelling pistols to
avoid focusing the eye of the opponent
has little foundation in fact. All forms
of English arms were becoming plainer
as a matter of general trend in taste by
the time the duelling pistol became
sufficiently popular to be distinguished
from the holster pistol

Social changes which include the passing of the Code of Honour, the increased relative efficiency of law enforcement agencies throughout the
world, the end of frontier regions and 'colonial areas', have combined to
reduce the need for handguns of all types, and the total demise of the
duelling pistol and the single-shot pocket pistol.

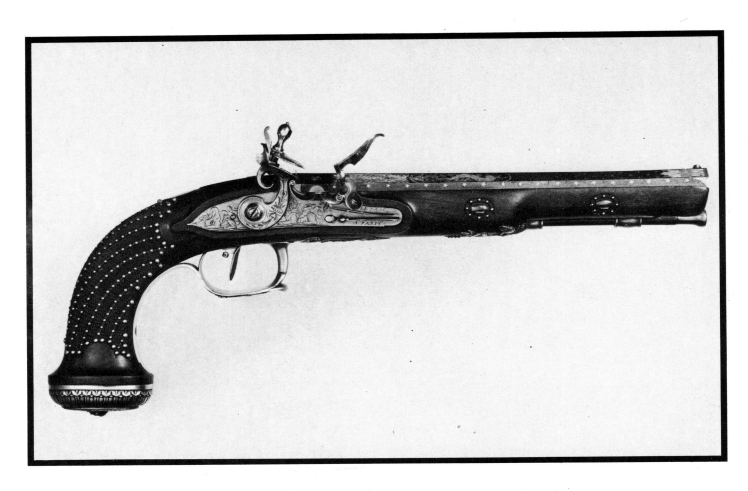

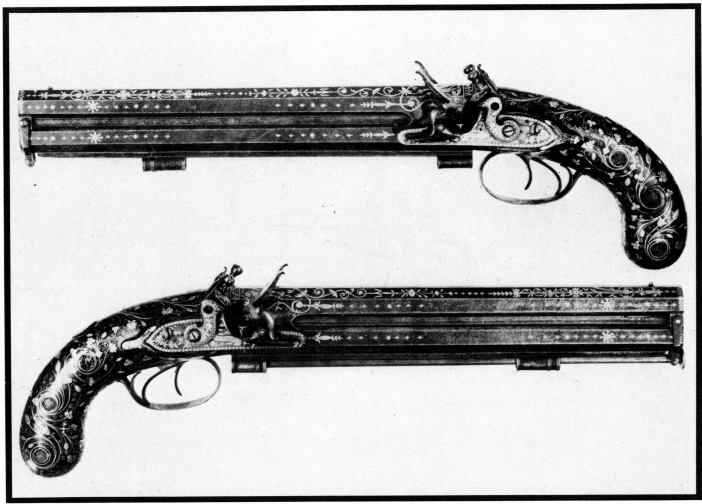

CHAPTER VI
DECORATIONS AND MARKS

LePage flintlock pistol decorated with small studs, inlaid barrel, and engraved lock plate

An unusual and heavily decorated pair of over/under flintlock pistols by · Manton

*Spanish gunmakers were renowned for the quality of their gun barrels and this French gun is fitted with barrels inscribed in gold 'IUAN PEDRO ESTEVA', a maker recorded as working from about 1700 to about 1740. The lock bears the name of the gun's owner 'NONNON 2*ME *COM*E *D'AR*RS*' who is recorded as joining the French army in 1791 and served in the artillery from 1808–11. He held the rank of quartermaster sergeant, being promoted to second lieutenant in 1815.*

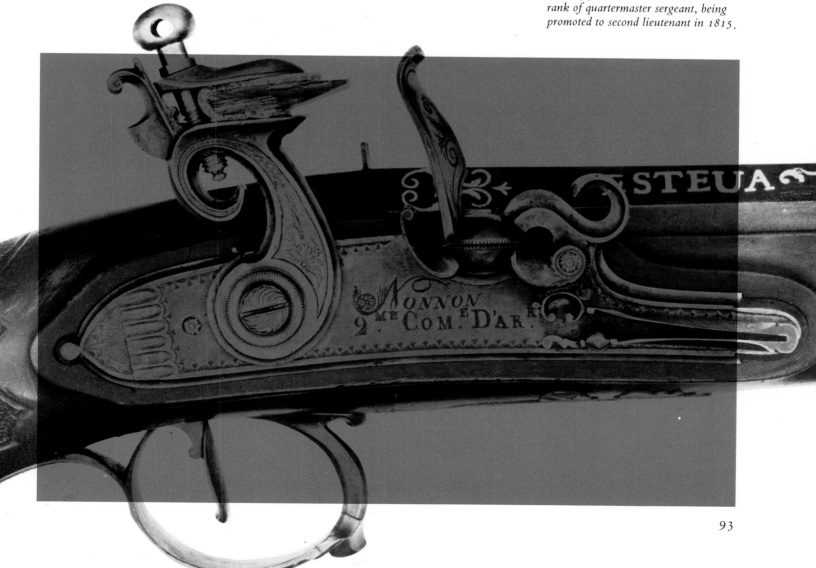

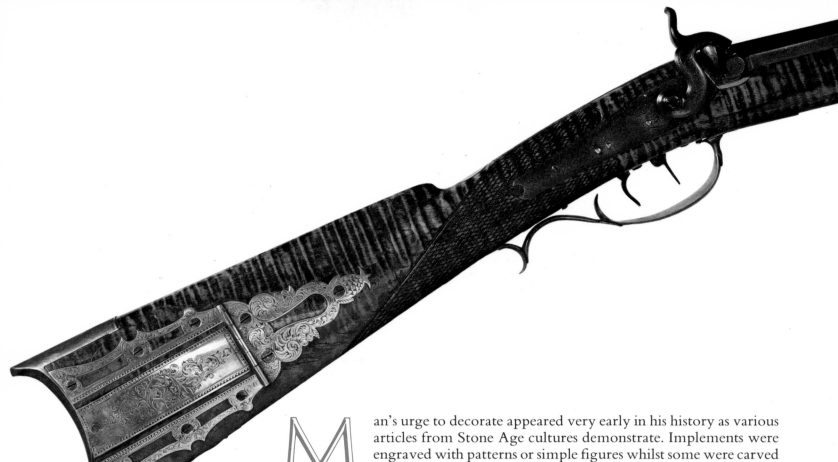

Peculiarly American is the Pennsylvania long rifle, often called the Kentucky rifle, developed by immigrant gunmakers from the European hunting rifle. Decoration was achieved by choice of attractively grained woods for the stock which is maple in this specimen. The lavish use of brass for fittings and patch box covers was common practice. This rifle was made, around 1840, by H. E. Leman, a gunmaker of Lancaster, Pennsylvania. A set, or hair, trigger which ensured a smooth, easy action when firing is fitted. Length of barrel 44.25 inches, bore .52 inches

M an's urge to decorate appeared very early in his history as various articles from Stone Age cultures demonstrate. Implements were engraved with patterns or simple figures whilst some were carved with skill and a feeling for the shape and composition of the material. There is abundant evidence, actual and documentary, to show that swords, daggers, spears, and armour were all decorated. For man, efficiency alone was insufficient – even for instruments of death.

On some of the earliest handguns there were embellishments and on one of the very few surviving specimens a head, probably intended to be that of Christ, is cast as part of the bronze gun. It must be admitted that this weapon seems to be exceptional for the majority of other surviving specimens are fairly crude and basic.

The diversity of techniques, skill in application and boldness in design of firearms decoration increased apace with the advance of man's technical ability to design, create, and manufacture more efficient weapons. For the gunmaker there were two materials with which he had to work, the metal in the barrel and furniture and the wood of the stock.

Barrel decorations. There were only two basic shapes of barrel, octagonal and round although, in fact, it was common practice to adopt an octagonal section at the breech, where strength was needed, and to convert further along the barrel to a circular section. There was scope for decorating the fore and rear sights and on a few fine quality pieces these were made from precious metal or chiselled into the representation of some appropriately shaped animal or figure.

The gunmaker had only a limited choice of materials and the vast majority of gun barrels were of brass or steel with brass favoured for sea service since it was less liable to corrosion. Although the gunmaker was limited in the amount of decoration, such as chiselling, that he could apply to the barrel there were techniques for embellishing the actual surface of the metal – blueing and browning. Rust was always a problem but blueing and browning effectively deposited a hard rust-resistant skin on the outside of the barrel which helped to preserve the metal.

Blueing was achieved by heating the barrel and then cooling it, the result bein a very satisfying blue coloration. Browning was achieved by chemical processes and mixtures with various formulae were applied to the barrel to produce an artificial rust. This coating was wiped off and the process repeated several times. As the action continued a delightful, rich brown skin was formed on the metal surface. At the appropriate point the process was stopped,

Made in Silesia, in about 1660, this flintlock sporting gun originally had applied gilt decoration on lock and barrel although some is now missing. The butt is almost completely covered with high quality staghorn inlay; each piece of inlay was cut to shape and placed in a corresponding recess cut in the stock. The principal figure, riding a camel, probably represents one of the Magi journeying to Bethlehem. Barrel 40.5 inches

This superb quality sporting gun was made by the famous French maker Boutet in his workshop at Versailles. The barrel is blued and has some gold decoration at the breech, the stock is finely carved overall with foliage, and the mounts are of silver. A pistol grip of ebony, fixed below the butt, is beautifully carved in the form of a caryatid. This weapon was probably part of a set which was made for Charles IV of Spain. Barrel 38.25 inches, bore .638 inches

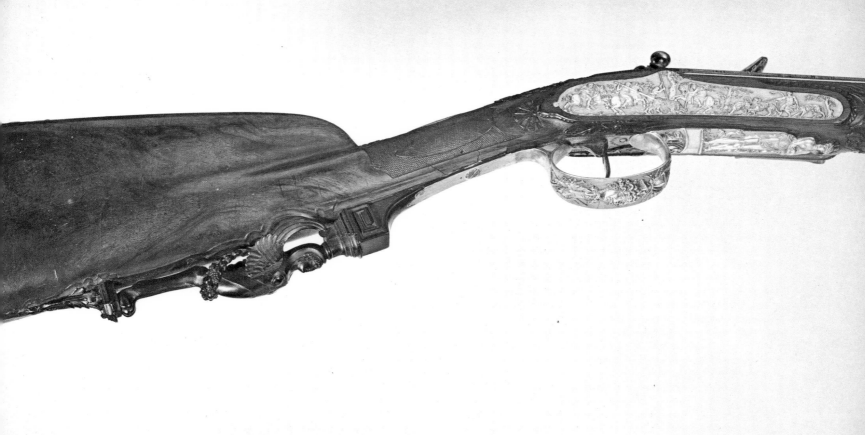

This snaphaunce lock is superbly chiselled overall with faces, grotesque shapes, and monsters. On the inner face of the lockplate is engraved the word 'BRENTO' – the name of a small village in central Italy which was at the centre of a thriving gun trade during the 18th century.
Length 6.2 inches

the barrel dried and given a polish. If the metal of the barrel had been striated or modified in any way during manufacture, browning had the effect of enhancing the different metal textures to produce a very attractive patterned surface. The effect of blueing was sometimes complemented by a process of gilding which deposited a thin layer of gold on treated portions of the barrel. This blueing and gilding was often used on swords but was less commonly applied to barrels of pistols.

Furniture decorations. The gunmaker had greater freedom of choice when decorating the other metal parts of the pistol, trigger guard, ramrod pipes, butt cap, lock, and escutcheon – the so-called furniture. As with the barrel, the most commonly used metals for the furniture were steel and brass although silver, gold, or combinations of these metals were used. In addition to a wider choice of material there were also greater possibilities for decorating the surface of the metal which could be cut much deeper and even pierced without fear of weakening a vital component.

The craftsmen of Northern Italy, particularly in the area around Brescia, were famous for the quality of their chiselling of steel and some Italian pistols with chiselled decoration are among the most attractive of all firearms. The buttcap offered a fairly large surface for the application of decoration and it was common to mould a grotesque mask at the base. The length of the spurs or arms extending up the side of the butt from the buttcap underwent a change in fashion and, as a generalization, it may be said that the shorter the arm the later the date of the pistol. Trigger guards, buttcap and ramrod pipes were occasionally decorated *en suite*.

Made in Vienna circa 1685 this pistol uses many forms of decoration. The barrel is of watered steel with inlaid gold plaques and is engraved at the breech with the figure of Hercules. Two gold plaques are inset in the lockplate and below the pan is engraved 'LAMARRE A VIENNE'. The steel and cock are chiselled with figures and all the steel mounts are engraved whilst the stock has gold inlay.
Barrel 13.9 inches, bore .65 inches

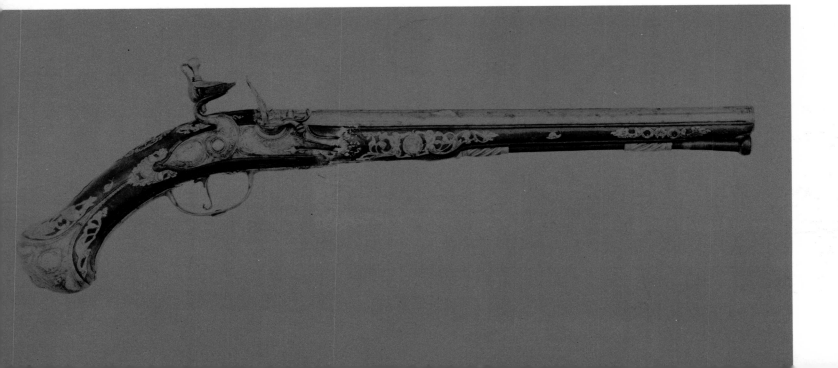

The lockplate with its large area afforded opportunities for embellishment. Certainly on the Italian pistols of the late 17th and most of the 18th Century, the lockplates were often beautifully chiselled, frequently with classical motifs. The cock itself might well be chiselled with simple high relief decoration and on occasions it was actually fashioned into the semblance of a head or a figure holding the flint. The frizzen itself normally attracted less attention from the decorator although many were chiselled or lightly engraved. The shape varied somewhat and, again as a general guideline, it can be said that the square-topped frizzen dates from the late 17th and early 18th Century except on Spanish firearms which retained this feature until much later.

Military pistols were seldom given the above-mentioned embellishments, the majority simply having an engraved line running around the lockplate parallel with the edge; a practice often repeated on the flat cock of the late 18th and early 19th Centuries.

Stock carving and inlay. Metal is, of course, not always an easy medium for decoration and the wooden stock was more commonly the subject of the designer's attention. Most European stocks were of walnut although other woods with an attractive grain were also used. In America maple was a popular substitute for walnut. In general, British firearms stocks were seldom elaborately carved although on early military pistols of the late 17th and early 18th Century there were small areas of carving around the barrel tang and lockplate. This minor concession to beauty was later omitted from the military firearm. On the continent of Europe the large surfaces of the wooden stock stimulated the instincts of the wood carver who often produced some quite elaborate effects. A common practice was to carve the lower part of the butt into the resemblance of some fantastic face. Sometimes pieces of a different wood were shaped and fitted to the stock.

One of the longest lasting methods of decoration was that of inlay and from the 16th Century onwards the use of horn, ivory, silver, and mother of pearl for inlaying butts of both long arms and pistols was common. Wheel–lock sporting guns, usually the property of some rich man with the taste and money to indulge his artistic whims, were often particularly elaborately inlayed with hunting and classical motifs.

A particular form of inlay practised very widely during the 18th Century

Although this flintlock sporting gun is engraved with the name 'F. Maddock Castel Yarde Dublin', it was almost certainly manufactured in France around 1685. Barrel, cock, lockplate, and butt cap are chiselled with classical motifs. Butt and stock are embellished with tracery, military trophies, and prisoners, all executed wifh silver wire inlay. Barrel 43.7 inches

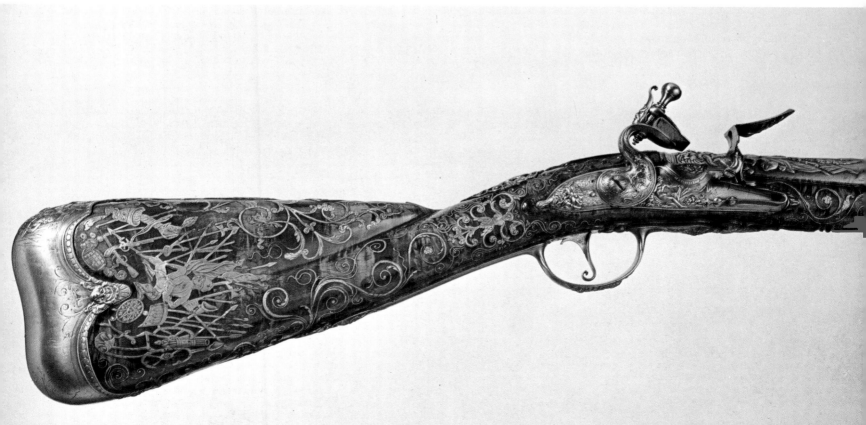

used silver wire and many of the so-called Queen Anne pistols were often heavily decorated in this style. Shallow trenches were cut into the wooden stock and into these were laid lengths of silver wire. The size of the trench was very carefully regulated and when the wire was in position it was gently tapped, forcing it to widen and so hold itself firmly in place. The most common style of silver wire inlay was in the form of spirals, volutes, and foliage patterns. Occasionally further decorative effect was afforded by hammering in silver-headed nails. The use of nails was a popular fashion with American Indians who often embellished the stocks of their long arms with brass-headed nails.

Wood was not the only material used for stocks and for a variety of reasons, practical or aesthetic, some gunmakers manufactured pistols with all-metal stocks. Some German wheel-lock pistols were made in this fashion and it was normal for Scottish pistols. Obviously the difference of material dictated different techniques and on most Scottish pistols decoration was normally limited to some simple engraving although on more elaborate and expensive weapons there might well be plaques of enamel or precious metal incorporated in the design. In the Balkans where metal-stocked pistols were popular, the local gunmakers delighted in embossing the entire surface with raised dots. It was also a common practice to bind the muzzle to the stock with plates or wire of copper or silver. In the Balkans and North Africa many pistols and some long arms were embellished by the addition of semi-precious stones to the stocks.

The advent of the Industrial Revolution with its increased use of mechanization did not destroy the demand for decoration. Percussion revolvers produced by Samuel Colt had the cylinders engraved with standard themes. The 1847 Dragoon revolvers showed a fight between Indians and soldiers; the Pocket Model of 1848 depicted a hold-up whilst the 1851 Model had a naval battle scene. Similarly the British Adams and Tranter percussion revolvers had some engraving on the sides of the frame. In the case of these latter weapons the engraving was executed by machine although a few were engraved by hand to customer's order.

Scottish weapons have always formed a special group both in method of construction and styles of decoration. This example of a 17th century Scottish longarm is very unusual in that the stock is fashioned of brass, engraved overall with scroll work. Another remarkable feature is the extension at the end of the butt; this is pierced through with the shape of a crown, suggesting a royal owner, possibly James VI of Scotland. The extension is removed by withdrawing the bar seen at the lower rear end of the butt

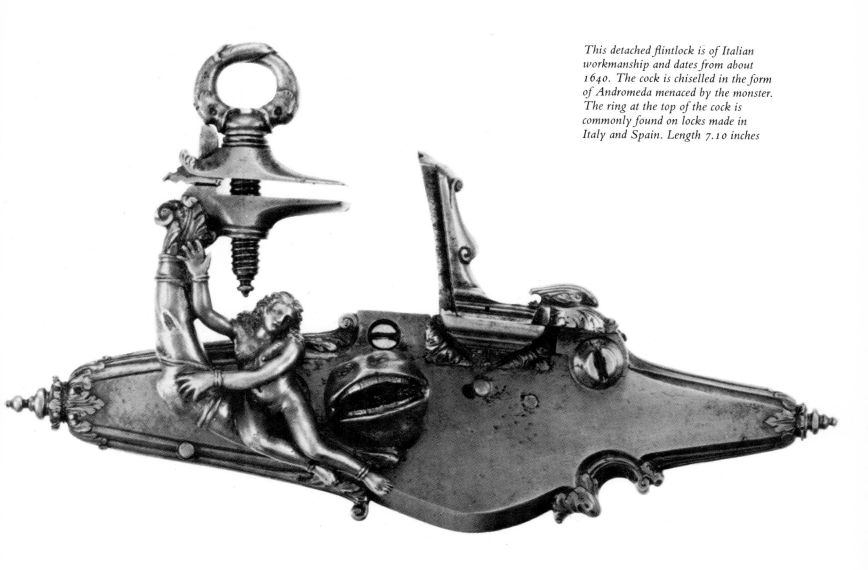

This detached flintlock is of Italian workmanship and dates from about 1640. The cock is chiselled in the form of Andromeda menaced by the monster. The ring at the top of the cock is commonly found on locks made in Italy and Spain. Length 7.10 inches

Gun marks. In addition to the applied decoration a great many firearms carried various marks, usually on the metal work, and especially on locks and barrel. Possibly the commonest of all are the makers' names or marks. On the majority of British firearms the maker's name will be found engraved on the lockplate or barrel. There was no standard practice, it depended entirely on the individual but generally speaking, the maker's name appears on the lockplate and his address on the barrel, most often along the top rib. In the case of British percussion revolvers the general usage was to put both name and address along the top of the frame and barrel. Samuel Colt used the same system although the details of the address he used did vary.

Since the barrels were of supreme importance certain rules were set down controlling their manufacture and sale. To ensure that the barrel was unlikely to shatter on the first shot it became established practice for gunmakers to submit their products for testing. Proceedure varied but generally it involved charging the barrel with a larger than normal load of powder. The charge was fired and the barrel was then examined for signs of damage; if it passed these tests a stamp was impressed on the barrel.

In Britain proving was done either at London or Birmingham. Birmingham proof was indicated by crossed sceptres, the precise pattern varying slightly according to the date. London used a crowned 'GP'. In Belgium, Liège was the main firearms centre and the mark used there was an oval with 'LEG' contained therein. Most countries developed their own systems and official marks although, strangely enough, the USA never did. In the case of British military firearms the contract system of supply used for many years,

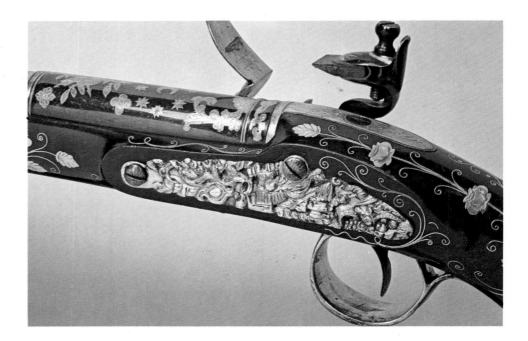

One of a pair of English flintlock holster pistols dating from around 1820-30. The barrel is decorated with blueing and gilding whilst the mounts are of silver-plated, cast brass. The stock is inlaid with German silver – a mixture of copper, zinc, and nickel. The barrel bears Birmingham proof marks. Barrel 12 inches, bore .66 inches

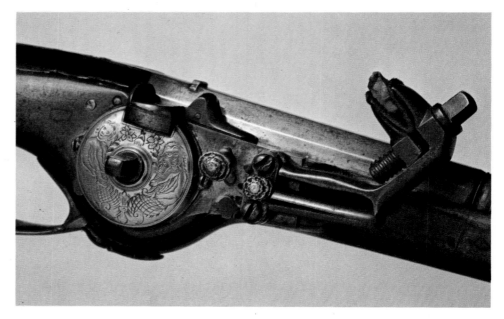

Even military weapons were often given a little decoration as on this wheel-lock pistol, one of a pair, which has the wheel cover gilded as are the pan release button and pivot of the cock. The stocks and other furniture in these pistols are quite plain and the weapons are typical of the military wheel-lock pistols of the early 17th century. Barrel 11.7 inches, bore .55 inches

involved the barrels being examined prior to proving and this viewing was indicated by a crowded 'v' stamped into the metal. Most civilian weapons seldom carried any marks apart from proof and the maker's name although with the later weapons, especially percussion revolvers, there was usually a serial number as well. Some weapons might also carry details of the patent covering the mechanism or design.

A very high proportion of sporting guns and many good quality flintlock and percussion pistols carried a small metal shield set into the butt. Known as an escutcheon, it was intended to carry the owner's name, initials, or coat of arms. Many surviving examples are of doubtful authenticity and Dr. H. Mayhew, writing in the middle of the 19th Century, described one man who encouraged the sale of his second-hand pistols by engraving them with spurious coats of arms. With the general adoption of revolvers presentation inscriptions and owner's names were most often engraved on the back-strap of the butt.

During the 17th and 18th Centuries there was a fashion for engraving mottoes on sword blades and this was also done, although far less frequently, on firearms; one favourite place being around the muzzle of a blunderbuss.

When the Royal Mail coaches were inaugurated in 1784 most of the guards' blunderbusses were identified by engraving around the muzzle 'HIS MAJESTY'S MAIL COACHES' and sometimes the number of the run was given as well.

Military weapons, as might be expected, usually have far more markings and, in general, the number is greater with more modern weapons. British military firearms, up until 1763, normally carried the maker's name on the lockplate and the word 'TOWER' and a crowned royal cipher and the date. After 1763 the date was omitted and only 'TOWER' and the royal cipher will be found. Regimental markings, usually very much abbreviated, were commonly placed on the barrel. 'R.H.G.' – Royal Horse Guards; '12L' – Twelfth Lancers, are fairly obvious but with the later cartridge weapons, '2 HLD. AC.R.F.A.' (2nd Highland Ammunition Column, Royal Field Artillery) is less easy to identify and figures usually indicate unit, battalion and number of the firearm on the inventory. Continental European military markings tend to be even more profuse and confusing. Long arms were also identified by barrel engraving although some regimental marks are often to be found on the top of the butt plate.

Another military mark to be found on many British firearms is the broad arrow, a device which has been used to identify government property for many centuries. Records of its use have been traced back to the mid 16th Century and until 1855 it is often found with the letters 'B.O.', Board of Ordnance, which, in that year became the War Department, 'W.D.'. This arrow and B.O. mark will frequently be found impressed into the wooden stock of military weapons.

The superb chiselling on the lock and barrel of this pistol is enhanced by the lavish use of gilding. Silver wire inlay decorates the stock and the butt carries an inset crowned monogram of the Empress Elizabeth of Russia. The lockplate is engraved along the lower edge with the date 1752 and the name of the great Russian arsenal 'TULA'. This pistol together with a number of other weapons was taken to France by Chevalier de Brulart in 1812 following Napoleon's disastrous Russian campaign. Barrel 11.6 inches, bore .6 inches

An interesting weapon both for its
superb inlay as well as its unusual
lock which is concealed within the
stock. Made about 1580, the carbine
has an octagonal, rifled barrel which is
comparatively short, only 24.3 inches
in length. The totally enclosed lock is
spanned by means of the spigot which
is accessible from the right hand side of
the stock. On the metal casing covering
the wheel is engraved the arms of the
city of Stettin. Barrel 24.3 inches,
bore .415 inches

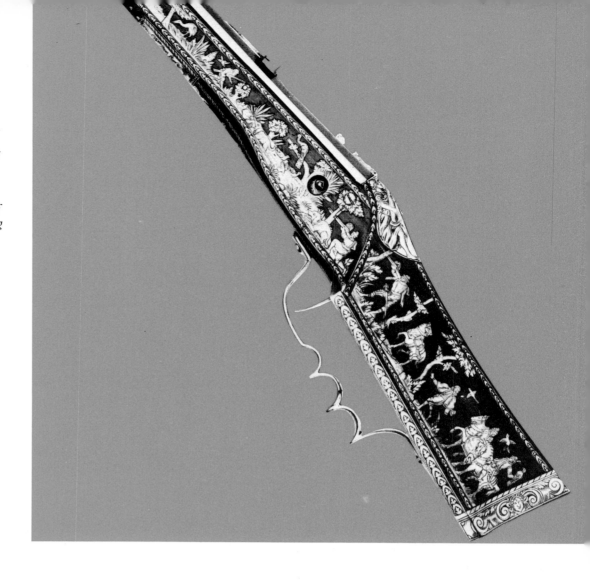

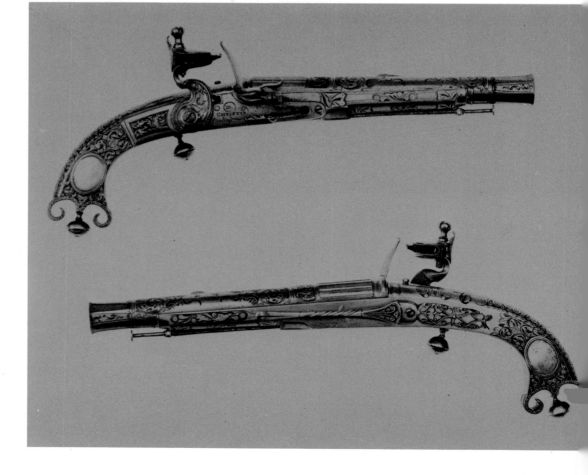

Pair of Scottish pistols made by
John Christie of Stirling circa 1755.
Most Scottish pistols of this period are
of all metal construction although few
are of such outstanding quality as
these. The ramshorn butts are decorated
with plaques and most of the surface is
covered with fine scroll work.
Ball triggers are another characteristic
of these weapons. Barrels 7.4 inches,
bore .64 inches

Certain commercial enterprises such as the East India Company, maintained their own military forces. Since they purchased weapons in bulk they were usually stamped with the company's mark, a quartered heart or a rampart lion.

Many flintlock and percussion pistols will be found to have file marks on the bottom of the barrel and on the inside parts of the lock. They are usually no more than a group of straight cuts and were placed there by the maker of the lock to identify the individual component parts during construction.

The profusion of marks, symbols, and names to be found on some firearms can prove both helpful and yet frustrating. The most comprehensive book is the monumental work of Johan F. Stockel *Haandskydevaabens Bedømmelse*. Although there are inaccuracies and omissions it is still the most generally useful book available for those who wish to delve deeply into this fascinating subject.

The standard of decoration on this revolver approaches the highest standards of decoration found on earlier flintlock pistols

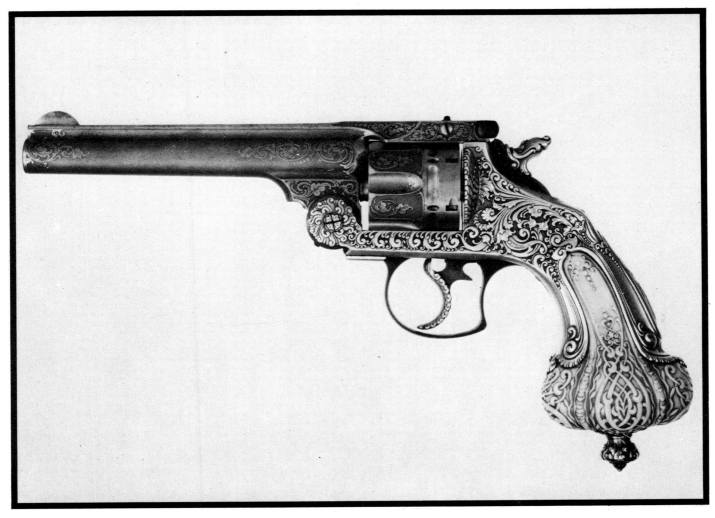

Facing page:
Print of 1845 showing early rockets used by the Royal Artillery in Britain

Above:
The US Civil War saw wide use of sharpshooters. This contemporary print portrays a soldier of the Union Army on picket duty at the Potomac

Right:
Sergeant Armstrong, champion shot of the British Army 1878-9, with breech-loading Martini action rifle

CHAPTER VII

NINETEENTH AND TWENTIETH CENTURY WEAPONS OF WAR

When, in 1807, the Reverend Forsythe produced his system of percussion ignition using fulminate of mercury, the door was opened for inventors to make such improvements to firearms that the subsequent hundred years saw more advance than the previous four hundred. The development of weapons has always depended on the development of ammunition, and once the simple and instantaneous percussion principle had been perfected several designs and ideas which had been abandoned as impractical with flint and powder ignition were resurrected to good effect.

One target of a multitude of inventors had been the production of a weapon capable of being discharged more than once, and a number of such designs had indeed been translated into reality in the pre-percussion days, but they were all carefully made by master gunsmiths and had to be equally carefully manipulated by expert shooters. They were by no means suited to the rough and tumble of the battlefield, but the robust simplicity of the percussion system now lent itself to more practical designs.

One of the earliest multi-shot systems was the pepper-pot revolver in which a group of barrels rotated around a central arbor, each bein presented to the hammer in turn. The earliest percussion version known is that made by Budding, of Stroud, England, in about 1830; in this model the barrels are indexed by hand before cocking the hammer, but within a few years the locks were designed to allow a pull on the trigger to cock and discharge the pistol, as well as rotating the barrel assembly.

Revolvers. The virtual father of the revolver as we know it today was, of course, Samuel Colt, who, with his patents of 1835 and 1849 secured to himself the monopoly of successful revolvers. The original Colt design was an open frame type in which the barrel was a separate unit attached to the frame ahead of the cylinder. This model was defective in that it was capable of firing a number of cylinders simultaneously, but by placing partitions between the nipples on which the percussion caps were fitted, this defect was cured, and the 'Paterson' Colt was produced for some six years until Colt went bankrupt. His fortunes revived however when the Mexican War began, and with some modifications suggested by Captain Walker of the Texas Rangers, production began once again with the model now known as the 'Walker' Colt. With the success of this weapon on the Frontier, Colt's future was assured and his name became synonymous with 'revolver'.

In England, after the expiry of the Colt patents, Adams produced a revolver which showed one considerable improvement over the Colt design; it was a solid-frame weapon, in which barrel, frame and butt were machined from one forging, thus producing an immensely strong weapon which could

7.65 Parabellum automatic pistol. More commonly called the 'Luger', this is the prototype model tested by the Swiss Government in the course of trials to determine its service pistol in 1900

Far right: the rare .45 Mars automatic, one of the most complex and powerful hand weapons ever made, compared with a US Army Colt .45 Model 1911. The Mars was not adopted as a military weapon, and after a brief commercial appearance it died by about 1903

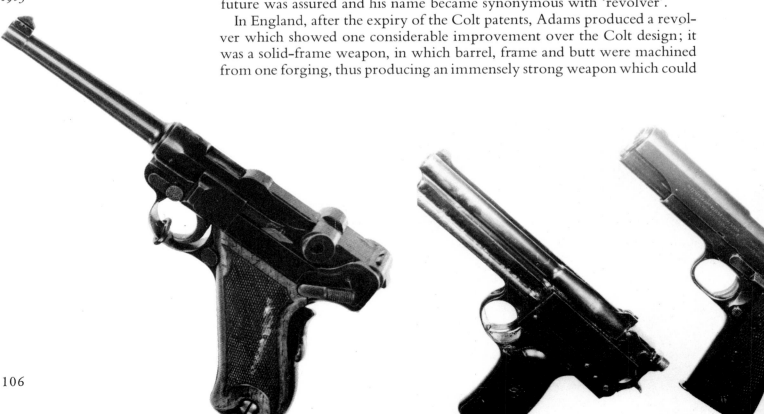

106

safely handle the most powerful cartridges, and this innovation was taken up by most manufacturers.

At this time the cartridge in use was still the powder and ball of the muzzle-loading era, but assembled into more convenient cartridges by confining the powder in a tube of paper or gold-beater's skin, with the bullet at the end either enclosed or attached by some adhesive. These cartridges were inserted into the front end of the chamber in the revolver cylinder, the bullet being forced home by the application of a lever rammer which formed part of the frame, and loading was completed by placing a cap on the nipple at the rear of each chamber. This was a tedious business, and, since Colt revolvers were easy to dismantle and remove the cylinder, it was the practice to carry about a second cylinder, ready loaded and capped.

But in 1847 a more convenient form of loading had been conceived by Flobert in France; he took the percussion cap as it stood and put a small lead ball in its mouth to make a short-range cartridge for parlour and gallery shooting. To simplify loading and unloading he placed a rim on the cap, and altered the shape until he finished with a rimmed case holding the bullet and with the fulminate distributed around the inside of the rim. He now produced a simple breech-loading rifle in which the rim of the case sat tight against the end of the barrel and was crushed by the falling hammer; this fired the fulminate and discharged the bullet.

For some unknown reason, Colt failed to appreciate the significance of this development and it was left to Smith & Wesson to develop a revolver to accept a metallic rimfire cartridge. To do this required that the cylinder chambers be bored completely through, instead of being 'blind' at the rear end, and by obtaining the patent covering this system of construction, they achieved an even greater stranglehold on revolver design than had Colt. Many and varied were the attempts to circumvent this master patent, but most were impractical, and those which sailed too close to the wind soon found themselves in communication with Smith & Wesson's lawyers.

The rimfire cartridge had many drawbacks, the principal one being its insecurity when used with heavy charges, and the invention of the centre-fire cartridge was the next major improvement. In this pattern the case could be made of more robust material – brass has usually been the favoured material, though everything from cardboard to plastics has been tried at one time or another – and only the central percussion cap needed to be of softer copper. Once the Smith & Wesson patent expired, in 1869, the last fetter was removed and from then on the design of revolvers simply became a matter of improvement of details. Indeed most of the improvement was over and done with by the end of the century, and advances in the revolver field since 1900 have been relatively minor.

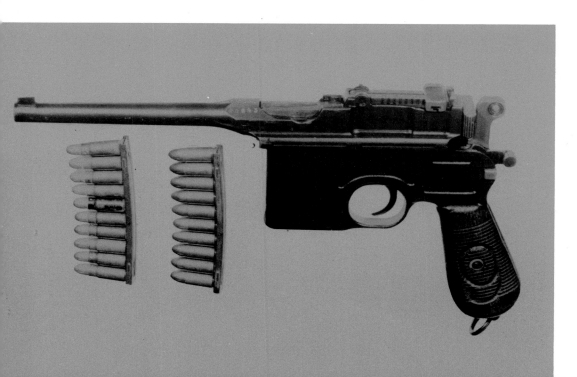

The Mauser Military Model of 1912. This model has been converted to 9 mm calibre during the First World War, and is so identified by the large '9' carved in the butt. The two chargers of ammunition are, left, the standard 7.63 mm rounds, and right, the 9 mm Parabellum rounds

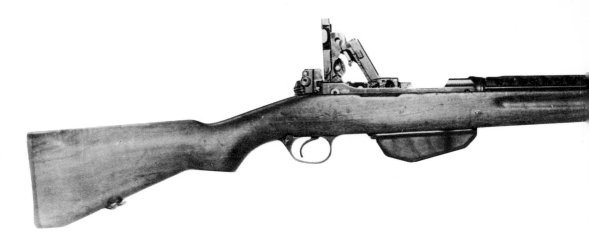

.276 Pederson rifle. Developed in the USA after the First World War, this uses a toggle-joint system of delayed blow-back operation. After exhaustive tests to select the new US Army rifle, it was declined in favour of the Garand

The first great milestone was, of course, the Colt Model 1873 or 'Frontier' Model revolver, that archetypal cowboy's weapon. It was simple, robust, accurate, and reliable, as witness its continuing popularity to this day. It was followed by the 1878 Double Action Government Model, a somewhat less reliable and successful weapon, and later by the 'Double Action Constabulary' or 'Lightning' Model. These were all of the type where a springloaded extraction rod beneath the barrel was used to eject the fired cases one by one through a gate on the right side of the weapon, through which, also one by one, fresh cartridges were loaded. This was a time-consuming performance, and a number of inventors set out to improve it.

It was left to W.C. Dodge to see that automatic extraction could be incorporated into the Smith & Wesson design of hinged-frame revolver, so that by the action of a cam as the barrel was tipped forwards, the extractor would be forced from the cylinder, ejecting the cases. This became a popular system, but it was viewed with disfavour by those manufacturers who preferred the solid frame class of revolver, and Colt, towards the end of the century, produced a model for the US Army in which the cylinder swung out from the frame on a crane arm, with a spring-loaded ejector removing the empty cases. Since then the side-opening revolver with solid frame has flourished in the United States, while the hinge-frame top-break pattern seems to have become almost a European monopoly.

In order to improve its issue handgun and have the benefits of the latest design innovations such as double-action locks and side-swinging cylinders, the US Army decided to re-equip, abandoning the single-action Model 1873 and adopting a Colt .38 model. The Philippine Insurrection quickly demonstrated that .38 calibre was insufficient to stop a determined – not to say berserk – native insurgent, and after a short digression into .38 Special calibre they returned to .45, adopting another Colt revolver.

Automatic pistols. But time was running out on the revolver. Although it remains in second-military service to this day, the 1890s saw the arrival of the self-loading or 'automatic' pistol. This again was an ideal to which many had striven, but not until the self-contained metallic cartridge had been perfected was there any possibility of making a practical weapon.

The first successful weapon of this class was the Austrian Schonberger. It is of considerable interest, since not only did it introduce the self-loading and self-cocking principles, but it also featured a breech-block locked to the barrel during discharge; it utilised the set-back of the cartridge primer on firing to

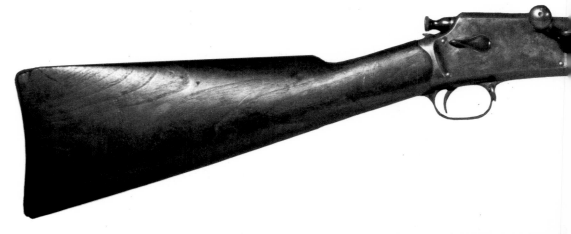

.44 Winchester-Hotchkiss Model 1883 rifle. Made by Winchester to the designs of Hotchkiss of machinegun fame, this was offered as a possible US Army rifle. The tubular magazine was in the rifle's butt-stock

unlock the breech; and it introduced a system of clip loading. For all its advantages though, the Schonberger failed to attain much commercial success, and specimens are exceptionally scarce today. The principal cause was the ammunition; in those early days quality control of pistol ammunition was negligible, and since a self-loader stands or falls by the reliability and consistency of its ammunition, the Schonberger was beaten before it started.

Contemporary with the development of the Schonberger, however, another pistol was in the design stage, a weapon which was to father a lusty and famous offspring. A German engineer, Hugo Borchardt, had spent several years in the United States as a gunsmith and engineer, working at one stage with Sharps on the development of rifles. His particular version of the Holy Grail was an automatic rifle, but he left his pursuit of this ideal to design a pistol. Failing to interest any American manufacturer, he returned to Germany and managed to sell the idea to Ludwig Löwe, a Berlin manufacturer.

More development work took place and, above all else, Borchardt appreciated the vital part the ammunition had to play in any automatic design, so he got to work to develop a cartridge which would operate smoothly and put up with the rough and tumble of automatic loading, and which would give repeatable consistency from shot to shot. Indeed, while the invention of the Borchardt pistol is commendable in itself, the development of the rimless bottle-necked cartridge, jacketed bullet and carefully formulated smokeless powder charge is probably Borchardt's greatest achievement. For the

Below right: Smith & Wesson New Century revolver, .455 calibre. One of 5,000 made in 1915 to a British Army order. An excellent weapon, but too good for the mud and filth of trench warfare, where its fine tolerances were often fouled, preventing the weapon from functioning

Below left: .45 Ballester Molina. Except for insignificant changes, this Argentine manufactured pistol is a copy of the US Army Colt .45 Model 1911

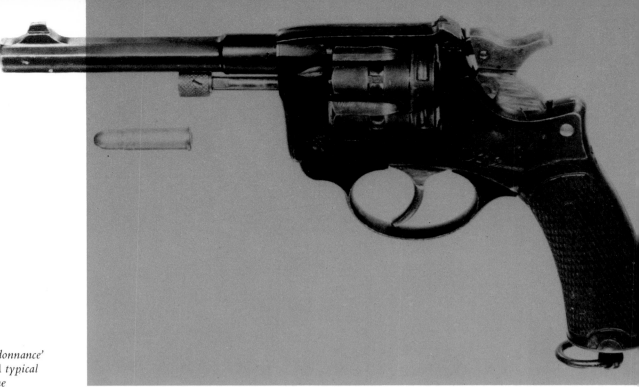

8mm French 'Model d'Ordonnance' revolver, model of 1892. A typical military revolver of the time

cartridge he so painstakingly developed later became the 7.63 mm Mauser and still later the 7.62 mm Soviet Tokarev, and as such it still flourishes.

The locking of the breech on the Borchardt pistol was done by a toggle joint system; the usual explanation of this system, for those who do not know it, is the analogy of the human leg. With the leg straight, pressure on the sole of the foot passes straight through to the hip. If the knee is bent, pressure will then bend it still further, allowing the foot to move closer to the hip. In the Borchardt, the foot is the breech block, the hip is the end of the barrel extension, and the leg and knee are the two units and joint of the toggle. When the breech is closed the toggle lies straight and the force of the exploding cartridge passes straight down to the attachment of toggle and barrel extension. The recoil causes the barrel, barrel extension and toggle all to recoil in one unit, but as they do so the toggle joint – or knee – is driven up by a ramp until it no longer forms a solid strut. At this point the movement of the barrel is stopped, but the breech block can continue to recoil, folding up the toggle and compressing a spring as it does so. When movement stops, the spring pulls the toggle back down, running the breech block back to the breech to chamber the next round and locking in place once more.

Borchardt introduced one other notable feature; he was the first to place the cartridges in a removable box magazine and then insert this magazine into the butt of the pistol. But for all its ingenuity, the Borchardt was less than perfect; it was awkward to handle, the mechanism was delicate and difficult to dismantle, and it was unsuited to military service.

Another employeee of Löwe, an engineer named Georg Luger, saw various flaws in Borchardt's design and set out to improve things, but Borchardt was no longer interested, having once more set out on the trail of his automatic rifle. So Luger carried on by himself and eventually patented a pistol of his own. Known in the United States as the Luger, Europe knows it as the Parabellum, a trade name developed for telegraph code purposes. The pistol was adopted by the Swiss Army in 1902 in the original calibre of 7.65 mm, using a fat bottle-necked cartridge.

It was tested by many other agencies, and one constant complaint was that the 7.65 mm bullet lacked the stopping power of the contemporary revolvers. Luger therefore re-designed his cartridge; he retained the base and body dimensions but opened out the neck to accept a 9 mm bullet. Retaining the body dimensions meant that the only part of the pistol which had to be changed was the barrel, since the breech block and magazine would work equally well with the new cartridge. This became the 9 mm Luger round, identifiable by its conical flat-nosed bullet, a Luger trade-mark developed in an attempt to improve stopping power.

The German Army accepted this 9 mm round and the pistol was formally adopted as the Pistole Model 1908 or P-'08, by which name it has always been known in Germany. Except for two pistols which were chambered in US Government .45 calibre and a .22 conversion kit made by the Erma Company, the Parabellum has only ever been made in 7.65 mm and 9 mm calibres, but a variety of barrel lengths have been produced and some minor variations made to suit the demands of various nations who adopted it from time to time.

One of the most notable variations was the German Army Model 1917 in 9 mm calibre, with an eight-inch barrel and shoulder stock and a special 32-round helical magazine. This was produced to arm machine-gun squads and other specialists during the First World War, an early stage in the development of the submachine gun. During the trials of this model it was found that the conical Luger bullet objected to being fed through the helical magazine and invariably jammed; the round-nosed bullet was introduced in its place and has remained the standard 9 mm Parabellum bullet ever since.

While Luger was busy turning the Borchardt into a practical proposition, a more famous name entered the automatic pistol arena. Peter Paul Mauser, who was by then well known for his rifles, had been attempting to produce a workable automatic rifle. The armies of the world, for a variety of reasons, were highly resistant to such a weapon, even when backed by Mauser, so he turned his attention to a pistol, since this seemed to have a better commercial chance. As it happened, his factory superintendent, one Herr Federle, had been amusing himself for some time with the design of an automatic, and this was taken as the starting point. The prototype was ready in 1895 and was patented in that year, and production of the Mauser Military Model began in early 1897; once finalised the design remained basically unchanged throughout the pistol's long life. The standard calibre was 7.63 mm, since Mauser took Borchardt's successful cartridge to save himself the trouble of developing another.

Just prior to the First World War a number of pistols were produced in 9 mm Mauser calibre, a cartridge longer and more powerful than any other 9 mm cartridge before or since, but the outbreak of war in 1914 stopped production and it was never revived. During the war, due to the shortage of P-'08 pistols, large numbers of Mausers were converted to take the 9 mm

The 7.65 mm Savage pistol. This American weapon used barrel rotation to lock the breech during firing. Although tested by the US Army in .45 calibre, its only official military adoption was in 7.65 mm by the Portuguese Army, during and after the First World War when its usual Parabellum pistols were not available

7.62 mm Soviet PPSh submachine gun. This simple weapon, turned out by the million during and after the Second World War, is the archetypal Communist weapon. Firing the Mauser-derived Soviet pistol cartridge and with a 71-round magazine, it has a formidable performance

Parabellum cartridge, but apart from these two exceptions, the Mauser Military has always been produced in 7.63 mm calibre. Large numbers were supplied to Russia, both during Tsarist times and to the Bolshevik forces in the 1920s, to the extent that the Mauser cartridge became the standard Soviet pistol and submachine gun round.

A notable feature of the automatic pistol scene in Europe at the turn of the century was the fact that almost every design of pistol came with its own design of cartridge, which could only be used in that pistol. This was due to the pious hope on the part of the designer that if his pistol was a success he could retire and live happily on the income from the subsequent ammunition sales. But in fact it usually meant that what was an otherwise promising design failed because the special ammunition was not easily available, and buyers turned to something they could feed more easily.

In the United States a similar situation had obtained in the early days of revolver development, but designers there were astute enough to appreciate the advantages of a few standard calibres, and when the automatic pistol business opened up, it soon settled down to a limited number of cartridge types. And the man most largely responsible for the design of these types was the man who put the automatic pistol firmly on the American map – John Browning.

Browning was well-known as an arms designer in the US but nevertheless had to go to Europe to obtain backing for his first automatic. With the assistance of Fabrique Nationale of Belgium he produced a .32 calibre blow-back pistol, in which the breech and barrel were not locked together on firing but relied on the inertia of the breech portion to remain in place until the bullet had left the barrel and the chamber pressure had dropped to a level at which it was safe to open the breech and extract the spent case. The success of this design was phenomenal; it has been estimated that over a million of these pistols have been made, and countless millions of imitations and 'Chinese

.45 Thompson M 1928 submachine gun. The well-known 'Tommygun' shown here with the box magazine

*7.62 mm Mauser Model 1898.
The German Army's standard rifle for
many years and typical of the Mauser
system as adopted by many nations*

*.303 Short Magazine Lee-Enfield
rifle, mainstay of the British Army for
fifty years, and one of the finest combat
rifles ever designed*

copies' were turned out all over the world in subsequent years.

Returning to the US, Browning interested the Colt company in the design of a heavier pistol suited to military applications, and in 1900 the Colt .38 automatic was announced. As originally designed this was a genuine automatic – once the trigger was pressed, the gun continued firing until the magazine was empty, a matter of but 1.4 seconds. As a practical weapon such a device is useless, since it cannot be controlled, as many other designers have discovered since then, and Browning rapidly changed it to the more normal self-loading single shot specification. This design was followed by hammerless pistols in .32 and .25 calibre, which, as well as being made in the US were produced by Fabrique Nationale for the European market. Then in 1905 Colt produced a .45 automatic which was an enlarged version of the .38 firing a newly developed .45 cartridge.

By this time the US Army was becoming disillusioned with the .38 revolver, and in December 1906 a board was convened with the task of determining a set of tests to discover 'a design of automatic pistol or revolver best adapted to fulfil the requirements of the military service'. In order to have one standard datum it was laid down that, to be considered, any weapon submitted must be chambered for the .45 automatic cartridge developed by Colt since this appeared to be an ideal military cartridge. Nine weapons, three of them revolvers, were submitted to the board, which delivered its report with commendable rapidity in April 1907.

After narrowing down the field to the Colt, Savage, and Parabellum pistols, the board submitted these to further tests and, as a result of its recommendations, 200 Colt and 200 Savage pistols were purchased and issued to selected units for extended trials. These showed that the Colt was marginally better, but still needed one or two minor modifications. These were duly

*British .45 De Lisle Silent Carbine.
A rare weapon, developed during the
Second World War for Commando
and other clandestine operations.
Based on the Lee-Enfield action, with
a built-in silencer, it uses the sub-sonic
.45 US Army pistol cartridge and was
the only absolutely silent long-range
weapon ever made*

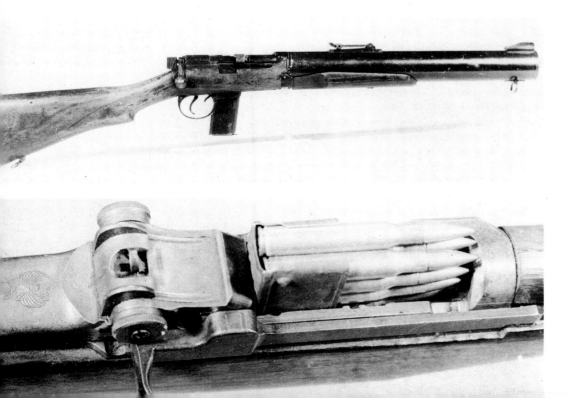

*.30 US Garand M1 rifle. This picture
shows the clip being loaded into the
magazine; when the bolt returns after
firing the last shot, the empty clip is
ejected. The badge engraved on the
receiver shows that this rifle was made
by P. Beretta of Italy for the
Indonesian Army*

9 mm Beretta Model 1918 submachine gun. Although resembling a rifle, with its full stock and folding bayonet, this is a normal blow-back submachine gun, and one of the earliest of the class

Centre: 7.65 Mauser Model 1934. Originating in a 1910 design which had been slightly improved over the years, this began life as a commercial design. Large numbers were taken into military service during the Second World War. The German Navy badge can be seen on the specimen shown here

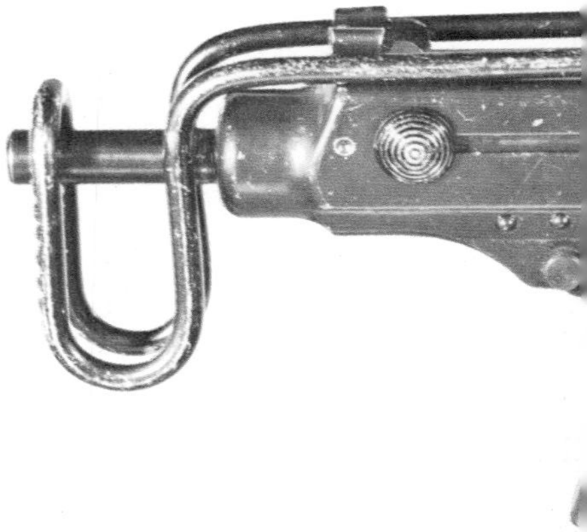

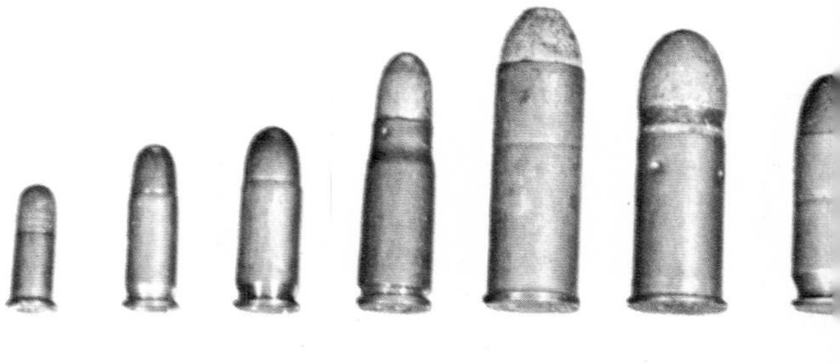

Pistol ammunition. From left to right: .22 Short; .25 Auto; .32 Auto; 7.63 mm Mauser; .45 Colt revolver; .476 Enfield revolver; .45 Colt Auto; .455 Webley revolver; .455 Webley & Scott Auto; .45 Webley 'Man-stopper'; 9mm Luger; 9 mm Parabellum; 9 mm Browning Long; 9mm Short

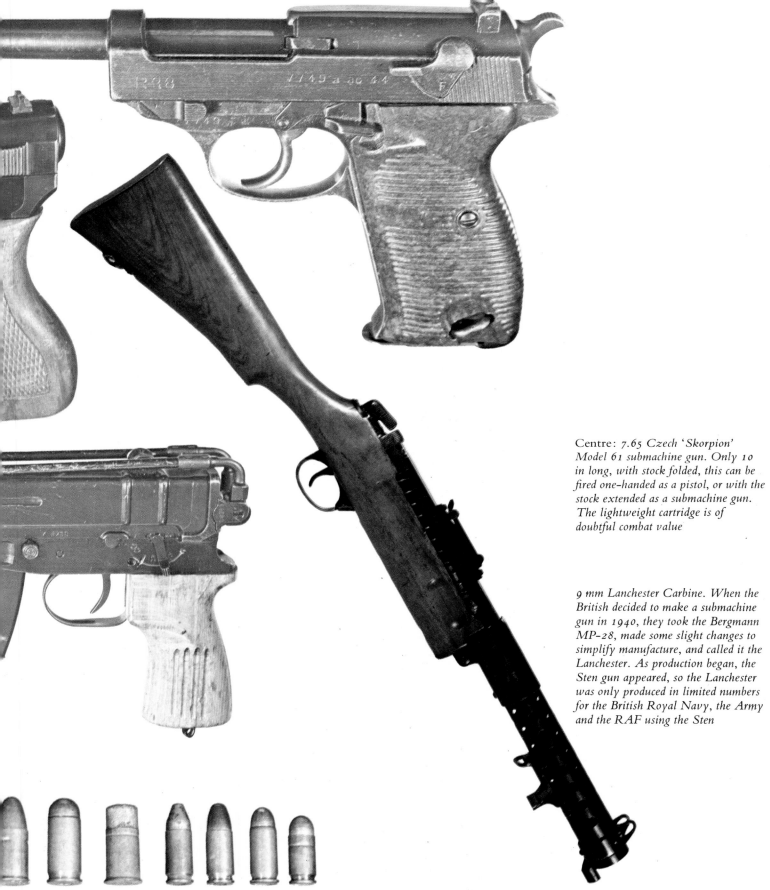

9 mm Walther P-38. Adopted by the German Army in 1938 to replace the P-08 Parabellum, the double-action P-38 has continued in military service ever since

Centre: 7.65 Czech 'Skorpion' Model 61 submachine gun. Only 10 in long, with stock folded, this can be fired one-handed as a pistol, or with the stock extended as a submachine gun. The lightweight cartridge is of doubtful combat value

9 mm Lanchester Carbine. When the British decided to make a submachine gun in 1940, they took the Bergmann MP-28, made some slight changes to simplify manufacture, and called it the Lanchester. As production began, the Sten gun appeared, so the Lanchester was only produced in limited numbers for the British Royal Navy, the Army and the RAF using the Sten

made, the pistol re-tested in 1910, and in 1911 it was officially adopted as the Model 1911.

Without doubt the US Government Model Colt automatic is one of the finest military pistols ever produced. Robust, well designed, simple, reliable, always well made of the finest materials, it has served the US Army well for 60 years, and bids fair to become the first centenarian in the military weapon field. After experience in the First World War a few small changes were made, causing the nomenclature to change to M1911A1, but it is fundamentally the same design as John Browning produced in 1910. Although .22 calibre conversions have been made to permit inexpensive target practice, the only different calibre ever made was a relatively small number of M1911 pistols chambered for the .455 Webley & Scott cartridge. These were specially made for the British Royal Navy and Royal Flying Corps during the First World War, and they remained in use in some cases until 1945.

The years of the First World War were a severe testing time for the weapons of the combatant armies, and their pistols underwent a thorough inquisition. By and large the lessons read were those the readers wanted to read; users of revolvers claimed that their weapon was hampered less by the muddy conditions, that it was more reliable in combat, and that it was less susceptible to variations in quality of hastily-produced wartime ammunition. The wielders of automatics declared that their chosen pattern was immune to mud and poor ammunition, carried more rounds than a revolver, weighed less, and so on and so forth. It is interesting to see that the Parabellum, whose operation is probably more dependent upon ammunition quality than any other weapon ever designed, remained high in German esteem, as well as being avidly sought as a souvenir by the victors.

After the war there was little advance in pistol design until the middle 1930s when John Browning's last design was put into production. Once more he had taken it to Fabrique Nationale of Belgium, who marketed it as the FN-Browning Model 1935. In 9 mm Parabellum calibre it was an improved M1911 in basic concept, its most outstanding feature being a magazine capacity of 13 rounds, a surprising handful. It was also fitted with an attachment point on the butt for a shoulder stock, a fitting which was popular in the early days of automatic pistols when it was hoped they might have a future as cavalry carbines, but one which had no place in the type of war fast approaching.

The German Army, assiduously preparing for such a war, decided that the Parabellum and the Mauser were unsuited to production in the quantity demanded, and began a search for a weapon which was easier to mass-produce, reliable, and less critical of ammunition quality. They found what they wanted in the Walther Heerespistole, a 9 mm weapon commerically marketed in 1937. This pistol had an unusual feature for an automatic in that the action of the trigger and hammer allowed double-action operation.

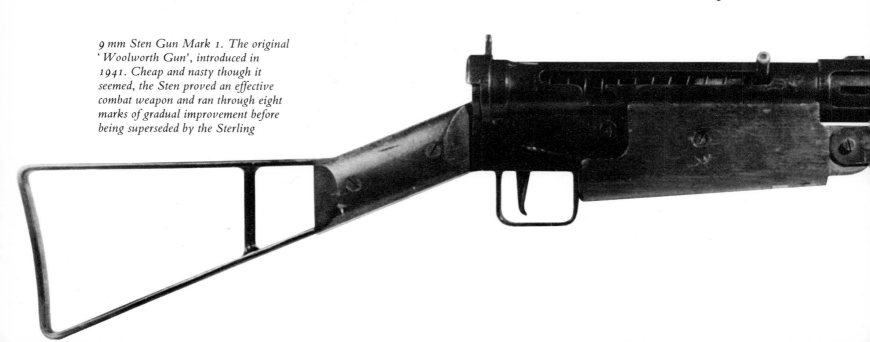

9 mm Sten Gun Mark 1. The original 'Woolworth Gun', introduced in 1941. Cheap and nasty though it seemed, the Sten proved an effective combat weapon and ran through eight marks of gradual improvement before being superseded by the Sterling

In the more usual automatic – the Colt, for example – the weapon is loaded by pulling back and releasing the slide, which loads a round into the chamber and leaves the hammer cocked. The user now has the choice of leaving it cocked and applying the safety catch or carefully lowering the hammer onto the firing pin, from which position it must be manually thumb-cocked before firing. The only other – and safer – option is to leave the weapon unloaded and pull the slide immediately before firing, a procedure which assumes the enemy will give you enough warning. In the Walther design the slide was worked in the usual way to load and cock; when the safety catch was applied it first retracted the firing pin and then released the hammer into the fired position. The safety catch was then pushed back to the 'Fire' position and the pistol holstered. When the need arose, it was simply drawn and the trigger pulled straight through; this first cocked and then released the hammer to fire the chambered cartridge.

The German Army adopted this as their standard weapon, calling it the Pistole Model 38, or P-'38, and production of the Mauser Military model finally came to a stop as the Mauser facilities were taken over for P-'38 production. Mauser continued to make the Parabellum pistol, principally for export, until 1943.

Since then little of note has happened in the pistol field. The double-action feature of the Walther has been adopted by many manufacturers and much work has been done in producing pistols with components such as the frame or slide made of light alloy. This can be a mixed blessing, since the pistol which is light to carry may be unpleasantly violent to shoot, since weight helps to cut down the recoil and allows more accurate shooting.

Submachine guns. From the beginning of the automatic pistol era, as already noted, there was a constant tendency to fit optimistic sights and shoulder stocks to pistols in order to convert them into something approaching a self-loading carbine. Though touted for military use, no military force ever accepted them and they were largely taken up by aristocratic game shooters. It is remarkable that none of their inventors ever took the further step of making the weapon fully automatic and turning it into a usable infantry weapon; though if one had done so it is open to doubt whether the military of the time would have accepted it. They had some funny attitudes towards machine guns in those early days.

In 1917 General von Hutier of the German Army helped to promote a new tactical movement in an attempt to loosen the grip of positional warfare which held the armies on the Eastern Front. He developed the 'Storm Troop' concept in which small parties of highly-trained and well-motivated soldiers could infiltrate defences under cover of fire and smoke. Such parties needed firepower in a convenient form; and the necessary weapon was forthcoming in the shape of the 'Bergmann Musket' or Machine Pistol Model 1918. This

.303 Martini-Enfield rifle. A good example of lever action applied to military weapons. Originally made in .455 calibre, these weapons were converted to .303 when the British Army adopted that cartridge, in order to extend their useful life

simple weapon is the ancestor of all the myriad submachine guns which have developed since then.

Operating on the blowback principle the Bergman Musket consisted of a seven-inch barrel in a perforated casing, a heavy bolt and striker, a cylindrical body holding barrel, bolt and return spring, and a wooden stock with a simple trigger mechanism. Its operation is simple to the point of crudity but it exhibits one essential feature which is frequently not grasped when considering these weapons, the system of 'differential locking'. This is a term invented to cover the method of obtaining some degree of safety in a blowback weapon by firing the cartridge while the bolt is still moving forward on its closing stroke. It sounds remarkably dangerous, but it is the heart of a system which permits heavy military cartridges to be fired from simple weapons.

The striker of the Bergmann is pushed permanently forwards by the action of the return spring, which lies between the bolt and the rear of the gun body. To operate the weapon, the bolt is pulled back until it is held by the trigger mechanism. A magazine, the 32-round helical type of the M1917 Parabellum pistol, is inserted into a housing on the left side of the body. When the trigger is pressed, the bolt runs forward propelled by the spring, collecting the top round from the magazine and pushing it into the chamber. Since the propelling spring is holding the firing pin forward of the face of the bolt, the pin and cap soon come into alignment and as soon as the cartridge meets resistance on entering the chamber, the pin contacts the cap with sufficient force to fire the round while the bolt is still moving forward and before the cartridge is entirely inside the chamber.

It follows from this that the explosion force and subsequent recoil of the cartridge has first to arrest the forward movement of the bolt and then reverse it, which gives sufficient delay to allow the bullet to leave the barrel before the bolt moves sufficiently far to extract the spent case. It is this system which allows the blow back principle to be used with a powerful cartridge, a relatively light bolt and a weak return spring; were the bolt stationary on firing, it would need to be heavier and have a much more powerful return spring to achieve the same results. Indeed, so safe is this system that it can be used on much heavier weapons; the 20 mm Oerlikon cannon has always relied on it.

Two or three thousand of these MP 18's were issued to the German Army in 1918 but the rest of the world failed to appreciate their significance, wrote them off as being peculiarly applicable only to the tactical situation obtaining on the Western Front in late 1918, and did little or no development work on them. The Swiss Solothurn company took over the Bergmann patents, modified the gun to use a more conventional box magazine, and produced it in small numbers, supplying them to several nations for test purposes.

In the US Army there was a body of opinion in favour of automatic weapons, derived from experience in France in 1917, and this party considered that the soldier should have some means of augmenting his fire-power during the assault phase of the attack. To provide this augmentation without the expense of providing completely new weapons came the Pedersen Device, a blow-back attachment which could be quickly substituted for the bolt of the Springfield 1903 rifle or Enfield 1917 rifle. Equipped with a 40-round magazine and firing a special .30 pistol cartridge, this conversion gave every man his own submachine gun at a moment's notice without involving much expense or change to the basic rifle; it could be converted back in 15 seconds to normal rifle functioning. The device was tested in France in December 1917 and enthusiastically reported on. Half a million, with 5,000 rounds apiece, were ordered to be ready for Pershing's 1919 offensive, but the Armistice called a halt to production. In the less heady atmosphere of post-war retrenchment it was more critically examined and abandoned.

Another American development had a better fate. The Thompson submachine gun, developed in 1919 as a police weapon, was later exported as a military weapon in small numbers, turning up in Ireland during the 'Troubles' and in Estonia during the Communist rising in 1924 among other places. But the Thompson's fame, rightly or wrongly, rests solidly on the Hollywood image, where it seemed that no self-respecting gangster or lawman could consider himself properly dressed without a Thompson in his hand. This popularity enabled the company to stay in business and in 1928 the gun was officially adopted by the US Marines. On the outbreak of war in 1939 numbers were hurriedly bought by Britain and France, and it was finally accepted by the US Army who kept it in service for some years after the war.

The Thompson had its faults; it was expensive, complicated, and difficult to manufacture; but it had one great point in its favour – it was reliable. Considered against some other submachine gun contemporaries, this one feature was enough to make it acceptable. As originally conceived it used a peculiar form of breech locking which claimed to hold up the blow-back action for a brief space to ensure safety; a locking piece connected bolt and body together and was so arranged at an angle to the axis of the barrel that the initial high pressure on firing would lock it solid but when the pressure dropped, after bullet ejection, it could move and allow the bolt to unlock. In fact there was an element of faith in this system, and after one or two brave souls had thrown away the locking piece and fired the gun with no ill effects as a straight blow-back, the US Army had an official redesign done to remove the lock and make the weapon simpler to produce.

.25 Colt Auto pistol. Not officailly a military weapon, though frequently carried by staff and senior officers in Continental armies, this is one of John Browning's most popular and most-copied designs

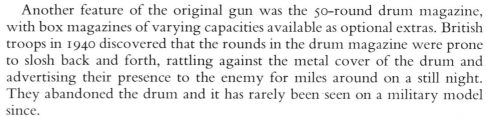

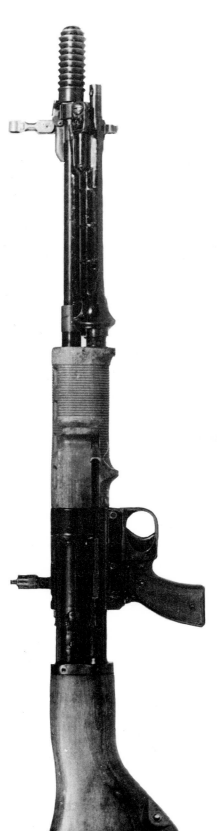

7.92 mm Falschirmgewehr 42. The German paratroop rifle, which, together with the MP43, has been the inspiration behind much of the subsequent development of assault rifles throughout the world

Another feature of the original gun was the 50-round drum magazine, with box magazines of varying capacities available as optional extras. British troops in 1940 discovered that the rounds in the drum magazine were prone to slosh back and forth, rattling against the metal cover of the drum and advertising their presence to the enemy for miles around on a still night. They abandoned the drum and it has rarely been seen on a military model since.

With the coming of war in 1939 and the unvieling of the 'Blitzkrieg' tactic, convenient firepower became a vital necessity. The German Army had paved the way by developing submachine guns in the late 1930s, adopting a design by the Erma company. This was taken into service as the MP 38, and when later modified to simplify production, the MP 40, but for some unknown reason the Allies christened it the 'Schmeisser' and this name has stuck; in fact Schmeisser, although designer of several submachine guns in his time, had no hand in this one, it being attributable to one Herr Vollmer. It is believed that, during the war, Schmeisser was managing a factory engaged in producing MP 38s, and a misunderstood intelligence report led to the confusion.

Britain began in the submachine gun field, after buying the Thompson as a stopgap, by making a direct copy of the MP 28, a design by Schmeisser which was more or less a clean-up of the original MP 18. The British version was called the Lanchester; it was used solely by the Royal Navy, and was a heavy gun which demanded some care in manufacture. It had originally been intended to equip the Army and RAF with Lanchesters, but while the factory was being tooled up, a design team from the Royal Small Arms Factory at Enfield, produced a cheap and cheerful weapon whose appearance caused traditionalists to retch but which worked. With little delay it was adopted for the Army and RAF as the Sten gun, and millions were made and distributed all over the world in the next few years.

The American equivalent of the Sten was the M3 or 'Grease Gun', another odd-looking weapon which, like the Sten, was drawn up with cheapness and ease of production uppermost in the designer's mind. Its final version, the

M3A1 was simplified to the ultimate degree – even the usual cocking handle was abandoned, and the gun was cocked by poking the forefinger into a hole in the bolt and hauling it back. Basically produced in US .45 calibre, by changing the barrel and bolt and putting an adapter in the magazine housing, it could be made to fire 9 mm Parabellum rounds, feeding from the Sten magazine.

The greatest supporters of the submachine gun were undoubtedly the Soviets. Faced with the prospect of arming and training vast numbers of men in the shortest possible time, and with a tactical doctrine which could be summed up as 'Get up, Get in and Get at, 'em' – which suits the submachine gun – untold millions of these were made in Russia during the war. Probably the best known is the PPSh, known familiarly in Eastern Europe as the 'Pepeshka', with the PPS 43 running it a close second.

The PPSh with its wooden stock, round magazine and perforated barrel cover was made familiar in countless war photographs, and has since been widely used by satellite nations. The PPS 43, which stemmed from a design produced in besieged Leningrad, is the epitome of cheap and effective design with its perforated barrel casing, curved box magazine and folding stock, entirely (except for the chromed barrel) produced from steel stampings and welded together, with no provision for firing single shots other than manual skill on the part of the firer. It was seen in increasing numbers as the war progressed, appeared once more in Korea, and turns up with monotonous regularity wherever Communism takes to arms.

By the time the war ended the submachine gun was firmly established as a standard weapon, and the designers set out to replace the rough and ready wartime efforts with something more refined; one of the drawbacks to rough weapons is that, although they may be highly serviceable and lethal, the soldier tends to regard them with distaste, feeling that he has been fobbed off with some sort of rubbish. And once troops lose confidence in their equipment, the end is in sight. So if for no other reason than morale, new submachine guns were called for. Hundreds of patterns have been proposed since then, scores tested, and a handful adopted. The British took up the Patchett-designed Sterling, which, to the soldier at least, seems to be the result of taking the Sten's action and clothing it rather more respectably to produce a much more acceptable and reliable weapon.

A more enterprising design is the Uzi, named after its inventor, Major Uziel Gael of the Israeli Army. This is an exceedingly compact weapon, yet carries a barrel of equal length to more cumbersome designs. The magazine fits inside the butt grip, another space saver, and the butt stock folds compactly away. The compactness is largely achieved by constructing the bolt so that a large proportion of it actually surrounds the barrel at the instant of firing, lying in front of the chamber and thus permitting a heavy bolt without demanding a large space behind the chamber to accommodate it. The Uzi is

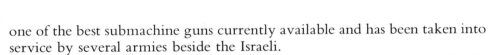

The .22 Fairchild 'Explorer' automatic rifle. Not a combat weapon but developed for explorers and also suited as a survival weapon for military aircrews. Firing the commercial .22 Long Rifle cartridge, it is a better game getter than the average combat weapon

one of the best submachine guns currently available and has been taken into service by several armies beside the Israeli.

Another postwar weapon of interest is the Danish Madsen. It was developed with an eye to production costs and is largely put together from simple pressings and stampings. It has a notable safety device in the form of a grip catch near the magazine which must be held depressed by the firer in order that the bolt may come forward to strike the cartridge. Unless the gun is held properly, it cannot be fired, and this device goes a long way to counter one of the most common (and dangerous) faults of the general run of blow-back submachine guns; due to the weak return springs, it is often possible to drop the gun on its butt and cause the bolt to be jarred far enough to the rear to pick up, chamber and fire a cartridge on the rebound. The early Sten was notorious for this fault, and most submachine guns have some form of safety notch for the cocking handle in order to try to prevent accidents of this nature.

Probably the smallest weapon of this class to be produced as a serious proposition is the Czech 'Skorpion' or, more properly, Model 61. This fires a .32 bullet, much smaller than the usual 9 mm Parabellum round which is the accepted standard among submachine guns, and of doubtful combat efficiency. Its size makes it of little value for long range shooting, but with the butt folded it can be fitted neatly into a holster and in emergency can be drawn and fired single-handed like a pistol. This feature and its lightness makes the weapon of particular interest to tank and aircraft crews, enabling them to have an automatic weapon handy at a minimum cost in weight and bulk.

Rifles. Finally we come to the third and most basic of the soldier's weapons, the rifle. The first military breechloaders of the modern era, the Prussian Needle Gun and the French Chassepot used a turnbolt mechanism to close their breeches, with a central firing pin, but this simple approach was abandoned as unreliable for many years, and designers developed weapons with sliding or dropping breechblocks controlled by under-levers – the many designs of Winchester and Marlin being the most successful.

Another famous system was the Martini, developed by a Swiss from an original design by Peabody, an American. The lever action Martini is immensely strong and also has the virtue of a very short 'lock time', the time between pressing the trigger and having the firing pin strike the cartridge cap. Because of this feature the Martini is still popular today among target shooters. Its strength attracted many designers of military weapons, since the military calibres of the day ran from .45 to .577 and a strong breech was vital. While warfare was carried on in the traditional way, with ranks of troops standing up to blast volleys at each other, the lever action was perfectly acceptable, but when soldiers began to lie down and take cover, the drawback of this action became apparent – it is difficult to operate a lever in the prone position – and the bolt action was revived.

Probably the most famous of all, and certainly the widest used, was the Mauser bolt action rifle. With the bolt locking directly into the barrel by lugs on its forward end, it is an exceptionally strong design, if difficult to keep clean, and being relatively foolproof it was accepted by innumerable countries as their standard magazine rifle. The United States after a short-lived flirtation with the Norwegian Krag-Jorgensen and the native Lee (with a

peculiar straight-pull bolt) adopted a modified Mauser design in their Sprin-field Model 1903 rifle.

By this time military rifle calibres had been reduced, largely due to the experimental work carried out by Major Rubin of the Swiss Army. He demonstrated that a small calibre jacketed bullet, propelled at high velocity by a charge of the new smokeless powder, was every bit as lethal as the old time lead bullet of large diameter, slowly pushed by black powder. Almost overnight, every nation fell into line and adopted a calibre in the neighborhood of .30 inch, together with a lead-cored jacketed bullet. England adopted the Lee Metford rifle, based on the American Lee turn-bolt and magazine, and then changed to the Lee-Enfield, which was simply a matter of changing the form of the barrel's rifling to one better suited to smokeless powder. The Lee-Enfield bolt used lugs at the rear end, locking into recesses in the rifle body, and is therefore theoretically inferior to the Mauser as a target rifle, but the speed at which the Lee bolt can be operated makes the Lee-Enfield a much better combat weapon.

7.62 mm Automatic Kalashnikov AK-47 automatic rifle. This Soviet design has been widely adopted among satellite nations. This version, with a forward pistol grip, is the Hungarian Army pattern

7.62 mm S.I.G. automatic rifle. This weapon can be used as a rifle, or, with the bipod in use and the full-automatic capability, can double as a squad light machine gun

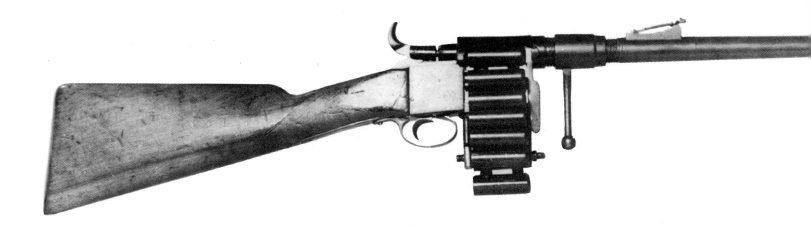

The Treeby Rifle, an early attempt at a multishot weapon. The chambers are on an endless belt and are fed to the breech in turn

Self-loading rifles. Once the automatic pistol gained acceptance among the world's armies, more interest began to be taken in self-loading rifles. The military mind tended to resist these weapons for a long time on the grounds of their complexity and their appetite for ammunition, and set up specifications which were practically impossible of attainment. While several designs were tried in small numbers during and after the First World War, the first really successful military self-loader was due to the farsightedness of General MacArthur, who authorised acceptance of the Garand rifle in 1932. Because of this action, the US Army was the only one to enter the Second World War with a self-loading rifle as first line standard equipment, and their success with it influenced the world-wide adoption of such weapons in the following years.

Germany had begun searching for a self-loader well before the Second World War and several models were tested until it finally came to a choice between a Walther design and a Mauser design. The Walther was finally accepted as the Gewehr 43; like the Garand it operated by using the gas generated by the fired cartridge, but the original designs, instead of tapping the gas from the barrel to drive a piston, caught it in a muzzle cap and then redirected it to operate a piston which in turn moved the bolt to eject and re-load. These were heavy and cumbersome weapons, and when it was re-designed into the final G-43, this clumsy system was abandoned in favour of tapping the gas off above the barrel to drive a short piston in direct contact with the head of the bolt. The G-43 was a serviceable weapon, but since it came on the scene half-way through the war, few were issued.

German airborne troops came under the control of the Luftwaffe and were not dependent upon the army for their weapons; moreover, as the apple of Hermann Goering's eye, they could ask for things which the army would never get. They demanded a light rifle which could also fire full automatic, since they felt that their specialist role demanded maximum firepower potential for every man. A design by Rheinmetall-Borsig was adopted as the Fallschirmgewehr 42 (FG-42), but the development work carried on after it was issued and it was still being modified and improved when the war ended.

The FG-42 was a very advanced concept and a very good weapon, but few were actually made. One drawback was that it was an attempt to build a lightweight weapon around a powerful cartridge, the standard German 7.92 mm rifle round. This round dated from the early years of the century when it was mandatory that an infantry rifle should be able to shoot to 2000 yards. In the latter years of the 1930s a number of German designers got together and took a long look at the rifle, what it was expected to do, and what it actually did. They came to the conclusion that the 2000 yard requirement was illusory, and that most infantry action took place at much shorter ranges – rarely more than 400 yards in fact. So they shortened the standard 7.92 mm cartridge and set about developing a new type of rifle to go with it. This was to be capable of sustained automatic fire or single shots. It would be light and easy to fire because the short cartridge would give less recoil. It had to be simple to make, cheap enough to throw away if it broke down, and sufficiently accurate up to the 400 yard limit.

The weapon they developed was turned down by Hitler, but unknown to him the designers had sufficient pull to get it into manufacture, calling it a machine pistol – MP 43 – by way of camouflage. After a successful debut on the Eastern Front, Hitler was converted and the MP-43 was accepted – though the Germans never bothered to change its title. It was the godfather of the class of weapon now generically known as 'assault rifles', characterised by their light weight, short cartridge, and selective fire capability. The rifle squad armed with these weapons has a fearful firepower at close range, but as anyone who has seen film of fighting in the Congo, Vietnam, Nigeria and similar affairs will have noticed, they do demand that the soldiers be properly trained, otherwise they simply become expensive machines for producing empty cartridge cases.

Perhaps the best known and widest distributed assault rifle in the world is the ubiquitous Kalashnikov or 'AK' of Soviet origin. Wherever Soviet influence extends, be it a satellite army or an unwashed pack of so-called revolutionaries, the AK will be there. After the German development of the short 7.92 mm cartridge and the MP-43, the Soviets appreciated the logic behind them and began development of a short 7.62 mm cartridge and rifle of their own. The AK is gas operated, with the piston above the barrel as in the German G-43. It uses a 30-round magazine and with its selective fire capability can serve as a rifle, submachine gun, or squad machine gun firing at 600 rounds per minute. Several variations exist, with furniture of solid or laminated wood, or plastic, with folding butts, wood butts, various types of sight, attached folding bayonets and other modifications, due to it having been made in Russia, East Germany, Czechoslovakia, China and other countries, each of whom made small changes to suit their own ideas. The latest version, the AKM, while resembling the AK, has the body made from stamped steel instead of being machined from a forging, a step which simplifies production even more. It is undoubtedly one of the most successful automatic rifle designs ever produced.

7.92 mm Maschinen Pistole 43. This German weapon, firing the short 7.92 mm Model 43 cartridge, is the forerunner of most modern assault rifles. This particular specimen is fitted with the 'Krummlauf' curved barrel extension and mirror sight to permit firing around corners

7.62 mm Simonov SKS automatic rifle. This Soviet rifle was a postwar design, using the short M-43 cartridge, but has been virtually superseded by the AK-47. With an attached bayonet, it is a gas-operated weapon of simple and reliable construction

With the AK, our survey of military hand and shoulder arms must come to an end. It would be rash to say that no major developments are likely, for at any moment an inventor may come up with a revolutionary idea which will change the firearms scene as did the percussion cap. At the moment the tendency is to reduce calibres so as to reduce the load on the soldier and allow even lighter weapons to be made; 5.56 mm (.223) is currently the vogue but work on development of even smaller rounds is in progress. Another field to be explored is the development of ammunition without the heavy and expensive metal cartridge case, a development which will relieve gun designers of the problem of extracting and ejecting the case, but which, in turn, will introduce some pretty new ones in the matter of sealing the end of the breech. Whichever way firearm design goes, however, it seems safe to prophesy that the movement will be prompted and oriented by ammunition development, as it has been ever since Forsythe's day.

ACKNOWLEDGMENTS

The publishers are grateful to the following individuals and organizations for permission to reproduce items from their collections (numbers refer to the pages on which the illustrations appear): Armee Museum, Ingolstadt: 11 (top), 14 (top), 18, 27, 39 (top), 87; Bavarian National Museum, Munich: 7, 15, 38, 39 (below); Bennett Collection: 100 (below); Christie, Manson and Woods: 17 (top), 22-3, 29 (top), 36 (top), 41, 42, 43, 44-5, 81 (below), 82, 83 (top), 84 (below), 89 (both photographs), 92 (both photographs), 103; Collectors' Arms Antiques: 51 (below); Crown Copyright – reproduced with permission of The Controller of Her Majesty's Stationery Office: Tower of London Armouries: endpapers, 8, 9 (all photographs), 12 (both photographs), 13 (both photographs), 16 (both photographs), 17 (below), 20, 21, 24 (both photographs), 25 (all photographs), 28 (both photographs), 32, 36 (left), 37, 40, 46, 48, 49 (all photographs), 52, 53 (both photographs), 93, 94, 95 (both photographs), 96 (both photographs), 97, 98, 99, 100 (top), 101, 102 (both photographs); Tower of London Study Collection: 50, 51 (top); John Freeman: 1, 4; Gower Guns, Hemel Hempstead: 65, 69, 72; Michael Holford Library: 55 (top), 105 Holland & Holland: 54, 73 (both photographs); Jagdmuseum Munich: 6 (left), 11 (centre and below), 14 (below), 19 (both photographs), 26 (all photographs), 30 (centre and below), 34, 35 (both photographs); Mansell Collection: 55 (below), 74-5; Mary Evans Picture Library: 104 (both photographs); Musée d'Armes de Liège: 61 (top); Royal Scottish United Services Museum, Edinburgh: 6 (right); Scottish Museum: 30 (top), 31, 76 (below), 80 (both photographs); Sotheby & Co.: 29 (both lower photographs), 33 (both photographs), 36 (right), 79, 81 (top), 85; Victoria and Albert Museum: 58, 59 (both photographs);

Other photographs are from the authors' private collections. Acknowledgments are due to Michael Dyer Associates for photographs taken throughout the book.

INDEX